D1541804

THE WHOLE MEAL

SALAD BOOK

THE WHOLE MEAL SALAD BOOK

by FRANCES SHERIDAN GOULART

Primus

DONALD I. FINE, INC.
NEW YORK

Library of Congress Cataloging-in-Publication Data

Goulart, Frances Sheridan.
    The whole meal salad book / Frances Sheridan Goulart.
        p. cm.
    Includes index.
    ISBN 1-55611-160-6
    1. Salads.   I. Title.
TX740.G66   1989   89-45440
641.8'3—dc20   CIP

Manufactured in the United States of America
10   9   8   7   6   5   4   3   2   1

To the people in my life who bowl me over—
my loving agent Ivy Fischer Stone,
my faithful secretary Esme O'Brien Carroll
and my menfolk—Ron, Sean and Steffan.

CONTENTS

INTRODUCTION

There are a lot of ways to improve your lot in life—and a lot of salads is one of them.

Calorie for calorie, salad foods contain more vitamins, more minerals, more fiber and more protein than any other food going. And what else qualifies as a diet food, a longevity food, even a curly green cure for constipation, high cholesterol and colitis? There is no better all-purpose food for good health.

Eleven million Americans may be diabetic, 30 million of us may be allergic to cow's milk, cheese and cream, 12 million of us may be vegetarians, and **40 million** of us may be too fat for our own good—but who among us can't eat a delicious salad and come back for seconds? And who hasn't got the time to toss? Life may be too short to stuff mushrooms, as someone once observed. But we've all got time to toss them into a salad and benefit from it.*

And these are certainly America's salad days. Per capita consumption of fresh vegetables rises five pounds every year. Serve-yourself salad bars, introduced in the 1960s, now offer as many as fifty to sixty items. Wendy's was the first fast-food chain to add one and Beefsteak Charlie's was the first restaurant chain. Supermarkets began installing them in the 1980s and discovered that it pays off. Up to 50 percent of all customers dig in.

We eat our salads in as well as out. According to government figures, America munches through 94.3 pounds of fresh vegetables per person every year—and more than a fourth of that total is lettuce. Demand for fresh salad has pushed annual individual consumption of lettuce from 17.5 to 23.8 pounds. Along with lettuce, we each ate an average of 12 pounds of onions (the second most popular fresh vegetable after lettuce), 10.8 pounds of fresh tomatoes, 8.1 pounds of cabbage, 7 pounds of celery, 6.8 pounds of corn and 5.9 pounds of carrots.

According to the United States Department of Agriculture, 20 percent of our total food dollar is now spent on vegetables and fruits—compared to only 15 percent for

*Mushrooms—now the #1 selection at salad bars—are a high-alkaline food. Foods high in alkaline help prevent food addiction and snack cravings. Mushrooms are also a good source of the anti-stress B vitamin pantothenic acid. Last but not least, a pound of raw mushrooms has less than 125 calories, the equivalent to only 5 large shrimp, with a cocktail sauce dip.

dairy products, 10 percent for baked goods and 2 percent for eggs.

Salads are in because dieting and health-consciousness are in. Old favorites such as peas, lima beans and potatoes are being by-passed in favor of lighter, lower-in-calorie mushrooms, radishes and celery, and more nutrient-dense vegetables such as dark leafy greens and broccoli. Broccoli consumption alone has tripled in the last 20 years. Today, it's our tenth most popular vegetable.

But a salad can be more than rabbit food for a dieter or health watcher. It can be a filling 4-star whole meal that is ready in half the time it takes to fix a more traditional (and calorie-laden) soup-to-nuts meal.

The idea of a leafy green meal in a bowl is nothing new. A favorite salad of England's Henry IV was made with diced boiled new potatoes and smoked sardines moistened with dressing and flavored with savory herbs. Mary, Queen of Scots, was fond of a salad of diced boiled celery root and lettuce dressed with mustard-flavored cream and garnished with chopped truffles, chervil and hard-boiled egg slices.

Composed salads were popular in Europe in the 1600s. One recipe in the *Cook's Primer* included everything from blanched almonds, raisins, figs, capers, olives, currants, red sage and spinach to roast beef, pickled eggs and quail.

But if you're going to join history's whole meal salad fanciers, you have to know how to combat the same-old-salad-and-salad-dressing syndrome. And here's plenty of help—a book full of whole meal salad recipes that need no more than a little something sprinkled on top or served on the side to become a complete lunch, brunch, dinner or supper. With the guide that follows, you can munch your way through a different salad every day, improve your health, lose weight and *never eat the same salad twice*. With the help of this book, your next chef's salad will be nothing like your last. You'll learn new ways to use common and uncommon greens, along with everything you've ever wanted to know about buying, storing, serving and even accessorizing America's favorite feel-good foods.

How To Make the Perfect Salad

1. *Buying.* Good greens come cheap, and great ones don't cost much more. To satisfy your green expectations, buy the best. Fresh greens should be crisp-looking and free of blemishes with no brown-tipped leaves. Head lettuces and cabbages should be firm and heavy for their size. Select all salad ingredients with care. Aim for a mix of colors, flavors, textures and shapes. After all, it's more than a salad. It's a whole meal.

2. *Cleaning.* A good salad is a dry one and a clean one. Greens that are too wet rot, and if leaves are water soaked, dressings won't stick. All greens and lettuces should be washed and dried carefully. For tight heads of lettuce and cabbage, you need to cut out the core by making a cone-shaped incision with a sharp knife. Then hold the head, cut side up, under running water. The water will push the leaves apart without bruising. Remove wilted outer leaves and drain the head well. Pat dry.

   Leafy lettuces (such as Boston and Bibb) should be cored, rinsed, then swished up and down in cool running water to remove all dirt or sand. Inspect each leaf to be sure it's squeaky clean. For other varieties such as escarole (a real dirt-catcher) or romaine, remove stem ends (the heart), discard any wilted or bruised outer leaves, then unhinge the leaves that are left one by one, and rinse each leaf individually to remove the dirt. Sprig greens such as parsley and watercress should be washed, drained and dried well, too.

   Drain all salad greens thoroughly and whirl dry in a wire basket, use a mechanical spin dryer or pat dry with paper toweling.*

3. *Storing.* Wrap greens loosely in soft toweling or plastic wrap, or put in a plastic bag but do not close tightly. Refrigerate until ready to use. Sturdy greens such as romaine and iceberg keep up to a week. Delicate lettuces have a two to three day life span. Cabbages are good for a week or more. For perfect crispness, greens need at least one hour of chilling before serving. When you're ready to use them, dry them once more so that no lingering water will dilute your dressing. What they say about oil and water not mixing is true.

*See "Equipment" (page 187). Another way to get clean greens dry without a gadget? Wash lettuce, put it into a pillowcase, close the top tightly with a rubber band, put the pillowcase with lettuce into the washing machine and turn on for the gentle spin cycle. You'll have dried uncrushed lettuce in no time. Variation? Use two bath towels that have been sewn together on three edges, or a large mesh-type onion bag.

4. *Other Ingredients.* Fast and fresh is the recipe for successful vegetable and fruit salads. They should be prepared and refrigerated just before using. Air, heat and light all destroy a salad's good looks, to say nothing of its nutrients. Don't peel or soak anything you don't have to. The greatest concentration of vitamins and minerals is in or just below the outer skin or peel, and many nutrient elements are soluble (and therefore lost) in water. Fruits such as apples, avocados, bananas and pears which become dark after cutting should be refrigerated in their dressing immediately, placed in acidulated water until ready to use or sprinkled with a natural antioxidant such as lemon juice or vitamin C powder until dressing is added.

5. *Serving.* Tiny leaves may be left whole, but large leaves should be torn or broken (cutting will bruise all but iceberg) into bite-sized pieces when salad is being prepared. Hand-torn greens also combine more readily with dressings and are easier to eat. How much salad is enough? Nobody knows better than you the appetites you're planning to satisfy, but a good guideline is as follows: For one adult whole meal serving allow 1 to 2 cups of greens plus ¼ to ½ cup of protein (meat, poultry, vegetarian protein, etc.) and have bread, crackers or rolls on the side. (If you're feeding marathon runners or teenage boys, all bets are off.)

To adapt a salad recipe serving two–three to feed four–six, simply double quantities of all ingredients except seasonings. Alter these to taste.

To make a salad more filling, increase the amount of meat, egg, cheese or Homemade Vegetable Protein (pages 35, 36), or try using a creamier dressing. You could also add a high-carbohydrate extra, such as a croissant. To make a salad more filling without increasing calories, add more raw vegetables or greens.

You'll find little agreement on what's classic in a salad or a dressing, but here's one of each to get you off and tossing:

Classic Whole Meal Chef's Salad

6 cups washed, dried and torn romaine lettuce
8 pitted black olives
1 ripe tomato in wedges
1 hard-boiled egg in wedges
  Thin slices of cucumber, to taste
⅓ cup julienned ham
½ cup diced or julienned cold chicken
½ cup julienned Swiss cheese (about 2 ounces)
  Classic Chef's Dressing with Herbs (following
    recipe)

• Place romaine in a large bowl. Top with olives, tomato, egg and cucumber. Arrange julienned ham, chicken and cheese around these.
• Spoon on dressing, toss lightly and transfer to chilled serving plates.

3–4 servings.

Classic Chef's Dressing with Herbs*

1 egg yolk, at room temperature
½ teaspoon salt or salt substitute
¼ teaspoon black pepper
¼ teaspoon minced thyme
½ teaspoon minced basil
⅛ teaspoon minced chives
¼ teaspoon minced tarragon
¼ teaspoon minced parsley
1 teaspoon minced shallots
¾ teaspoon minced garlic
2¼ teaspoons Dijon-style mustard
½ cup vinegar
1½ cups salad oil

• Place the egg yolk in a blender or food processor and add all remaining ingredients except the oil.
• Cover and blend. Add the oil very gradually, blending continually during and between additions.

Makes 2 cups.

*Omit the herbs and this recipe will double as mayonnaise.

How To Make Composed Salads

You don't even need a recipe for a salad if you have a formula. To make what's known as a *salade composé* (composed salad—one that is arranged on a platter rather than tossed in a bowl), here are some possibilities:
• Leftovers such as roast beef, steak, veal, fish, chicken or game.
• Vegetables such as cooked potatoes, beans or rice; fresh peas; young spinach leaves; tiny beets, cooked and sliced; baby whole zucchini; raw mushrooms; red peppers, charred and skinned; cauliflower or broccoli broken into flowerets and blanched; slices of red onion; black olives; hard-boiled eggs, quartered and sprinkled with fresh herbs; or tiny pieces of pimento to put on top.
• Canned, fresh or frozen seafood such as sardines, shellfish and even baby lobster tails.

COMPOSED SALAD GROUND RULES

• Don't chop pieces too small.
• Don't mix too many ingredients.
• Don't toss everything into a mushy mess.
• Do arrange attractively.
• Consider using 2 dressings instead of one: Use a vinaigrette to coat the vegetables, and if pieces of chicken, fish or meat are on the salad menu, make a mayonnaise or other creamy sauce to serve separately at the table.

Making a Whole Meal Salad

If you're making a habit of salad, make a habit of filling your salad bowl right. What does this mean in terms of choosing ingredients? It means for an adult female between 19 and 50, a complete meal in a salad *should* provide the following (a little more of the works for a male or a growing kid):

Calories	683*
Protein	14.7 g
Vitamin A	1333.3 IU
Thiamine (B₁)	.35 mg
Riboflavin (B₂)	.416 mg
Niacin (B₃)	4.5 mg
Vitamin C	20.0 mg

*Lettuce alone provides an average of 20 calories per loosely packed cup.

Vitamin D	2.08 mcb
Vitamin E	7.2 mg
Calcium	266.7 mg
Magnesium	100 mg
Iron	6.0 mg
Phosphorus	266.7 mg
Potassium	1250.0 mg
Sodium	600.0 mg
Zinc	5.0 mg

If your salad's typical, it isn't well-balanced. The average made-in-America salad is either a dainty high-sodium side dish or a calorie-overstuffed feast. The average salad for one either provides a skimpy 150 calories or a hefty 600— but with less than 10 percent of an adult's daily protein requirement and more than 100 percent of that person's need for vitamins A and C.

If you're serious about salads because you love them a lot or because you count yourself in the one out of four Americans on a do-or-die diet, your salad bowl probably suffers from other nutrient and calorie underloading or overloading.

An appetizing plate of fresh fruit and cottage cheese does look healthy, but it falls short of being a nutritious whole meal. While it boosts your vitamins A and C intake, it doesn't deliver enough of the important minerals deficient in many women's diets. And it doesn't come close to satisfying a woman's thiamine and magnesium needs, either. It probably contains 300 calories—too scant for a whole meal, especially if you skimped on breakfast.

Salad blooper #2 is the salad that packs too much punch. Throw in meat, eggs, croutons, cheese, several raw vegetables, lettuce and lots of Thousand Island dressing, and you've got a go-for-broke 800-calorie-plus meal. That's at least 20 percent too many calories, with triple the protein you need, four times the vitamin C, six times the A and twice the sodium recommended. This isn't a whole meal, either; it's a meal and a half!

What to do if you want to do it right? Forget about calculating minerals, such as sodium and phosphorus. They're as easy to come by as calories. And since you're using fresh greens and fruits and raw vegetables, you've got your vitamin A and C bets covered, too. Both vitamins E and D are supplied by the ingredients in any good salad oil or dressing.

So what does that mean that you're likely to leave *out*

of your whole meal salad? Calcium, iron and zinc, essential minerals of which the average American diet tends to run short.

Good salad sources for these essentials? There are plenty, but you'll never know you've found them without a scorecard. "Feeding Your Salad" (page 177) is just that. And you'll never get them if you stay in an iceberg-and-romaine rut. If you switch from iceberg to Swiss chard, for example, you'll get four times more iron. And if you use the new-age greens such as radicchio, amaranth, field lettuce, arugula and the Chinese cabbages, you can boost not only your iron but also calcium and overall vitamin input up to four times. (Tip-off: The greener the green and the redder the red, the more nutrients there are.)

How about protein and zinc? No problem if meat, poultry, fish or dried beans or nuts appear on your menu. There are 15 grams of protein in 2 thin slices of lean roast beef or a 2-ounce cube of Swiss cheese.

But what if you're very vegetarian and don't even eat cheese? It's still possible to maintain a healthy diet, but you must be careful to add enough protein sources. There's at least a little protein in almost everything: Even a potato, carrot and fresh corn salad can satisfy a third of your daily protein needs if it goes into the bowl with a dark green, and even more if a whole grain or raw nuts and seeds are added.

Good ways to beef up protein? Add meatless meats (see recipe for Homemade Vegetable Protein #1 and #2) or cheese, or a high-protein salad dressing (egg-, yogurt- or cheese-based dressings can boost protein by as much as 9 grams per serving). And for B vitamins and calcium, homemade dressing tops anything you can buy ready-made.

Each whole meal salad in this book provides a meal's worth of essential nutrients for a healthy adult. Calories? With the exception of just a few salads, the recipes that follow provide a square meal's calories (500 to 700). To raise or lower calories, simply add to or subtract from the suggested topping, greens or spread. And if you follow the serving suggestions after each recipe or if you add a few extras from the "Feeding Your Salad" scoreboard, you can give yourself additional green bonuses.

GLOSSARY OF GREENS AND OTHER INGREDIENTS

Greens

Lost your head over lettuce? It's easy to do. But don't do all your tossing with iceberg. Among the other "true lettuces" are butterhead or semihead lettuces, looseleaf and Cos. (The semiheads or Boston and Bibb types are easily recognized by their broad, buttery leaves and their succulent flavor.)

But a lettuce lover's life isn't complete without a variety of greens—including cabbages and mustard greens, unusual-tasting greens such as arugula and sorrel, and wild greens such as dandelions. So here's a guide to the common and uncommon greens to keep that leafy love affair on the front burner.

Amaranth.   Also known as summer spinach or Chinese spinach, amaranth was one of the staple foods of the Aztecs. It is cultivated in the Far East and in the tropics, but can be grown in any sunny backyard. It surpasses broccoli and potatoes in nutritional value, supplies more calcium and vitamin C than spinach, kale or lettuce, has only 10 calories a bunch and is richer in protein than other greens. A rare spinach-flavored treat in raw or cooked salads. If you can't find it, grow it. (See "Mail Order Sources" for where to buy seeds.)

Arugula.   Not a lettuce, but a mustard green, arugula is also known by its English name rocket, or roquette. In Europe, especially around the Mediterranean, arugula is prized for its peppery, pungent and distinctive flavor which increases as the plant matures. If you like watercress or radishes, you'll like arugula. Best combined with a lettuce such as romaine, endive or Bibb, arugula is sometimes sold as an herb. If you grow your own, pick it young while it's sweet; older leaves are bitter, and once flowers appear it becomes a weed. Arugula is considered an astringent salad green, which means it helps to depress the appetite.

Beet Greens and Swiss Chard.   Both have a spinach-and-beet flavor and taste best lightly steamed in hot coleslaw or in wilted or room temperature salads. Botanically speaking, these nutritionally potent greens are closely related. Swiss chard is a type of beet which does not develop the bulbous root of the beet, and it is grown for its edible leaves which are broad and crisp and vary in color from yellowish to dark green (there is also a rhubarb chard with crimson stems and wine red leaves). Cooked, the flavor of Swiss chard is delicate and spinach-like. Indeed, chard makes a good spinach alternative. Chard was a green commonly used by the Greeks, Romans and Chinese. Why it's called Swiss nobody knows, including the Swiss themselves.

Bibb Lettuce.   A member of the butterhead family of lettuces, these deep green little heads have been called the world's most luscious lettuce—elegant and expensive, very tender, rich and tasty. All Bibb lettuce was homegrown until 1900 when a Louisville gardener started producing and selling it to small groceries. Bibb lettuce today is grown in California, Ohio and New Jersey and shipped all over the country. To a connoisseur, heads grown outside Kentucky may seem too large and blowsy. The Bibb still grown in Kentucky looks like an elongated dark green rose with a light green, crisp core. The texture is unique (not soft). The reason? Kentucky Bibb is grown in limestone soil.

Bibb is a good bet for home gardeners and it will even grow in a window box outside your kitchen or office for instant "windowsill salads" (see "Tips" at end of this section). The two best bets for home gardens: Burpee Bibb, close in taste to the original, can be started indoors in flats and transferred as seedlings to the outside, or sown directly; or summer Bibb, developed to be grown outside even in the hottest months.

Bok choy (Chinese Chard, Chinese Mustard, Brassica Chinensis).   A cluster of thick, broad-based white or greenish-white stalks with loose, broad dark green leaves that look more like chard than cabbage. A light, delicate flavor; crisp texture. May be steamed like spinach or cut into bite-sized pieces and stir-fried. The hearts only should be eaten raw. The small ones are tastiest.

Boston Lettuce.   A fragile, small, soft-headed member of the butterhead family, the packed tender leaves are green on the outside, yellow within. The butter-sweet subtle taste can be a substitute for the higher-priced Bibb.

Broccoli Rabe.   Rabe, raab or rape is really a Roman cabbage. If you're a Brussel sprouts eater, this is the green for you. Like turnip greens, the leaves with their broccoli-like buds have a pungent flavor, so a little goes a long way.

Use in hearty, full-flavored salads. A substitute for arugula or cabbage or mustard greens—and vice versa.

Cabbage. A member of the bigger-than-big Brassica family, which includes kale, collards, broccoli, cauliflower, Brussels sprouts, turnips and kohlrabi. Compact-headed cabbage comes in many varieties and colors—firm or loose, with plain or curly leaves, in shades of white, green or red. Cabbage is ancient: the Roman poet Cato recommended it raw as surpassing all other vegetables in value. (Raw cabbage with vinegar is still recommended as a hangover cure.) Of the cabbages generally available, Savoy has the mildest flavor.

Cabbage may be shredded or grated and eaten raw in salads, or steamed or stir-fried and eaten cooked, hot, at room temperature or cold. Refrigerate cabbage unwashed in a plastic bag. Cabbage may be substituted for kale, turnip or mustard greens or broccoli rabe.

Chicory. The extremely curly edged leaves, shading from dark green to a bleached blonde interior, give chicory its other name, curly endive. Its texture may be reminiscent of steel wool, and the flavor is a bit bitter, but it makes a good addition to any mixed salad bowl. If you make an all-chicory salad, use enough dressing to make it palatable.

Chinese Cabbage (Celery Cabbage, Napa). Long, large, oval, compact shape—pale green with white frilly but crisp leaves. A crunchy cross tastewise between cabbage and celery. Combines well with all common lettuces. Use raw or steamed and chilled. May be used in place of celery or bok choy.

Corn Salad. So called because it grows wild in cornfields (it can be cultivated in the home garden, too), corn salad is also known as lamb's lettuce or mâche.

The plant is four to six inches tall with leaves that are spoon-shaped or round, smooth edged or slightly toothed, growing in compact rosettes. It is extremely popular in Europe, where it is sold on street corners in bunches like flowers.

Try it alone or combined with arugula, radicchio or spinach. A taste-alike substitute if you can't find corn salad is escarole.

Dandelions. A spring green, familiar by its yellow buds in lawns and along country roads. For salads, the younger and smaller, the better—the leaves should be picked before blooms appear to be at their delicate best. The slightly bitter taste makes dandelions a plus in a bowl of mixed greens. Delicious in wilted salads with creamy dressings, the vitamin A-rich dandelion buds make good garnish or crouton substitutes. Dandelion greens may be substituted in recipes calling for endive or chicory, and are less expensive too.

Endive (Curly-leaf). It's a leafy green with a slightly bitter flavor best combined with blander or sweeter salad greens. Endive grows in a loose head, with crisp, narrow white or rose-tinted ribs and ragged-edged leaves. The leaves circle a yellowish heart (another type of endive is escarole, with straight, broad leaves). Both are members of the chicory family along with Belgian endive. (Endive is often sold as escarole or chicory, confusing salad makers further.) Two other endives are the cicoria San Pasquale with dandelion-like leaves, and a delicious peppery radicchio. Use as you would chicory and count on the same calories and nutrients.

Belgian Endive. Also called witloof or French endive, the large, tender sprouts of this plant are shaped like pointed cylinders, four to six inches long and one inch across. With tightly packed creamy white leaves ending in pale yellowish-green tips, they are slightly bitter and crisp. (The root is used to produce a coffee substitute.) Not cheap, but one pound provides twelve endives, enough for four whole meal salads. Four calories an ounce and tasty filled with any soft cheese, dip or your choice of 30-Second Salad Spreads (page 156).

Escarole. Another member of the chicory family, also called broad-leaved endive or chicory escarole. Escarole leaves are broader and less curly than conventional chicory. Flavor is somewhat bitter but pleasant. Escarole's dark green exterior leaves and golden interior ones make it a perfect background for composed salads with cheese, meat, nuts or fruits. If you tire of escarole, look for its taste-alike, corn lettuce (mâche).

Fiddlehead Ferns. Fiddleheads, so called because, unopened, they look like the end of a violin, are the coiled young fronds of ostrich ferns or bracken, plucked when four to eight inches tall (after that they turn bitter). Popular in Canadian salad bowls, fiddleheads are a crop flavored between tender green beans and asparagus. Delicious steamed and chilled with a vinaigrette or combined with any leaf lettuce. Available fresh only in the spring, many gourmet shops sell canned fiddleheads.

Iceberg Lettuce.   All crisphead lettuces can be traced back to ancient Babylonian days. Today's most popular crisphead lettuce, iceberg, was a favorite in Asia Minor. Head lettuce was a common item on supper tables in sixteenth century Europe and in America, it was one of the first vegetables planted in every colony.

Eighty percent of the iceberg we eat today comes from either Arizona or California. How did it get its name? Prior to modern refrigerated produce trucks, it had to be packed for traveling in ice-layered crates. The two types of iceberg found most often are Imperial (large, thin, cabbagelike crumpled leaves) and Great Lakes (thick, dark green leaves with a tough texture).

Nutritionally, iceberg is at the bottom of the lettuce list, but the greener it is, the better a source of vitamins A, B, C and E it is, as well as of iron, phosphorus, potassium and calcium.

Iceberg and all other crispheads may be shredded, cut in slices or cut into wedges and dressed, or cored and stuffed whole for a salad for four. Separated leaves may be used for individual spread-and-munch snacks.

Kale.   Kale is a kind of "wild" cabbage with floppy, tough, curly-edged leaves. Two blue-green varieties are grown in the U.S., and both are robust in flavor. Best used thinly slivered or well torn if raw, and in combination with soft lettuces. It's even better when steamed and chilled in wilted salads. May be substituted for cabbage, collard, mustard or turnip greens.

Leaf Lettuce.   Also called garden lettuce, this is a group of soft, delicious lettuces which do not form heads but grow as leafy bunches. They come in a wide range of colors—from fresh green to red or oak-tipped to bronze-tipped. Fragile with delicate flavor. Toss with care. Good as a solo green or in any mixed salad.

Mustard, Turnip and Collard Greens.   These members of the cabbage family have a pungent, delicate flavor especially prized by the Chinese, Italians and Southeastern Americans. Young greens are a tasty addition to mixed salads. But the flavor is hot, so a little is a lot. They combine well with sweeter leaves such as spinach or romaine. Richer in vitamin C than citrus fruit, these provide 500 percent more calcium than does common lettuce. Buy only bright green bunches.

Oakleaf Lettuce. A picture-perfect lettuce with notched leaves that are soft and smooth with a delicate flavor. May be substituted in recipes calling for any leaf lettuce. Don't overtoss.

Radicchio. A chicory at a price. Also known as Rosa di Treviso, the small, sturdy, cabbage-like head has ruby red leaves and white ribs and veins. Some varieties are long, resembling romaine. Known for its mildly pungent, radish-like taste, it is good raw (or steamed and chilled) and tossed, or in mixed salads to accent more familiar lettuces. May be substituted for chicory or vice versa.

Romaine. Also called Cos lettuce, this is a crunchy all-around salad green that keeps well. Romaine has a distinctive long oval shape with dark green outer leaves that shade to yellow inside. Succulent, juicy to the bite, good alone or in any combination. Like iceberg, head and leaves may be stuffed.

Sorrel. The young, tart, lemon-flavored tender leaves of sorrel (also called sour grass, sheep sorrel or French sorrel) are prized in salads by Europeans. Leaves are arrow-shaped, and make a good contribution to either crisphead or loose-leaf salads. Related to the wild green dock, sorrel will thrive in any backyard. The vitamin C-rich leaves which are famous for their thirst-quenching properties make a good lemony-ade. Use sorrel as a substitute for grated lemon or lemon juice or as an alternative to watercress.

Spinach. The broad, crinkly, sweet, tender leaves make good, raw salad greens. The leaf stems are sweet and edible when young. Spinach originated in Persia and was introduced in the U.S. in 1800. Any recipe with "florentine" in the title is a tip-off that spinach is one of the ingredients.

Spinach will sweeten a salad. It also adds color to pale salads made with escarole, endive, cabbage. And Popeye's favorite green is the third best leafy green source of vitamin A. Spinach begins to perish after only three days of refrigeration. Buy it fresh and crisp, wash it well and use it fast. Spinach may be substituted in recipes calling for Swiss chard or beet greens.

New Zealand Spinach. This tough customer is not a true spinach. It's highly nutritious but an acquired taste because of its bitterness.

Watercress and Garden Cress. Watercress is a peppery

member of the mustard family. The plant grows best wild in running water or in springs and streams. The Persians, Greeks and Romans ate it for pleasure and for better health, and at one time it was considered a cure for mental illness.

Used largely as a garnish, it makes a first-rate salad green all by itself. Buy it young, fresh and bright green. Like to grow your own cress? The easiest to grow on windowsills is pepper grass—a pungent, curly-leaved variety. You can sprout garden cress seeds bought at a health food store. Watercress may be substituted for arugula, radicchio, or used in place of radish sprouts or sorrel.

Wrapped in cloth or paper towels and refrigerated in plastic bags, sturdier lettuces such as iceberg and romaine keep up to five days, while butter and leaf types have a two-day life span.

Other greens such as as cabbage are usually good for a week when refrigerated unwashed in a plastic bag.
Grow your own, and your salad days need never end. Here's how.

HOW LONG WILL IT KEEP?

• What to grow? Forget iceberg and most head lettuces; they're tough to grow and take too long. The ideal indoor lettuce, which can be harvested in six weeks, is oakleaf. Other choices are ruby, green leaf, butterheads and Bibb. (Ask your nursery owner about the new miniature varieties.) As long as there is no direct draft, lettuce grown in a cool place or close to the cool mini-environment of an air conditioner during the summer months will produce an abundant crop, but four hours of more-or-less direct sunlight is necessary. Some varieties are not as sun-greedy. Again, ask at your nursery. Even better, invest in a grow light.
• Plant one variety every week until you have six or eight pots of lettuce going. (You can get a dozen 8- to 10-inch pots into a single bay window.) Harvest outer leaves as they grow (except with Bibb varieties, where the whole head is harvested once grown). A continual harvest keeps your salad bowl filled every day. Best vegetable bets for a hanging pot? Golden Cherry or Tiny Tim tomatoes, dwarf bell peppers or cucumbers. And if you want decorations

TIPS FOR INDOOR SALAD FARMERS

you can eat, don't forget nasturtiums. There are three basic types of nasturtium plants: dwarf, semi-trailing and climbing. Colors range from garnet and scarlet to orange and yellow. Sow seeds inside in January and you'll have hanging baskets by April. Sow in October and you'll have ruby red blossoms for Yule. A favorite variety? Whirlybird.

• Parsley and cress are both good for a pot, but you'll need lots of pots. Pick the leaves regularly. They grow almost all year 'round. Replace plants every eighteen months.

• Use water-filled pebble trays beneath all your pots. Atmospheric moisture is essential to preventing spider mites.

• Moist (*never* soggy) soil is the key to a crisp, healthy crop, whatever you plant. On warm days you can open the windows for some air circulation, but avoid drafts.

• Don't crowd your edible plants. They need all the nourishment their roots can gather. Use fresh, rich potting soil and fertilize regularly.

• To discourage aphids, make a soap-bubble insecticide from a little liquid soap and lots of water.

TIPS FOR OUTDOOR SALAD GARDENERS

• The easiest greens to grow are chicory, spinach, arugula and corn salad.

• Old-fashioned row-by-row layout is good, but a hexagonal arrangement of equidistant seedlings is better.

• Salad crops are 95 percent water so they need rich soil with high organic content. Improve yours by raking a two- to four-inch layer of peat moss or compost on top and digging it in. And just before seeding, add a complete garden fertilizer.

• Most salad crops can be seeded directly but for Bibb-type lettuce, set out seedling transplants.

• Salad green seeds need cool soil to germinate, and cool nights to grow. Once they sprout, sunlight's an essential.

• Plant other seeds at the same time, and don't use all your seeds at once. Sow partial rows or areas every two to three weeks so your harvest will keep coming.

Other Ingredients (See "Salad Dressing Ingredients" [page 123] for oils, mustards, vinegars and basic seasonings.)

Anchovies. Flat or rolled, packed in brine or oil, anchovies add an appealing, salty richness to salads and dressings. A good garnish. Anchovy paste makes a tasty dressing ingredient.

Bamboo Shoots. Love artichokes and they're not in season? Here's an alternative.

Cardoon. If you favor the flavor of artichokes, oyster plant (salsify) or bamboo shoots, then cardoon's for you. This celery-colored Mediterranean relative of the artichoke is most often used in Italian and French salads. String, chop and blanch it before using as a salad ingredient.

Carrots are compatible with anything you add to a green salad, even fruits. Use them raw or cooked, in sticks, circles, slivers or grated. They add sweetness, color, crunch and vitamin A to the bowl.

If you grow your own carrots, put their phosphorus-rich leafy tops into your bowl, too. Carrots in their second year of growth bear delicate white flowers like Queen Anne's lace, another salad bowl extra.

Celeriac (celery root, celery knob, celeri-rave). A special variety of celery grown for its irregular, globe-shaped roots. Remove the rough brown skin and use the whitish flesh. Steam or boil and chill, or grate raw. Has an intense celery flavor with smoky overtones. Low in calories. Keeps one week refrigerated.

Celery. In the ancient world, celery was prized as a medicine as well as a flavoring and food. There are many varieties but the two most often sold in U.S. markets are Pascal and Golden Heart, the latter blanched to produce stalks with light, whitish golden color and yellow green leaves.

Celery is a good source of fiber but a poor source of nutrients. Good in salads raw or cooked, there are only 17 calories per cup. To use, separate stalks, trim leaves and remove any strings with a paring knife before slicing, mincing or shredding. Use only the inner stalks for salads. The fresh leaves add a concentrated flavor to dressings. To dry leaves for future use, spread on a cookie sheet and dehydrate in a 225° oven until crumbly. Store in an empty spice jar.

Cucumber. The green "fruit" from a trailing vine of the gourd family. Use raw, peeled or unpeeled, plain or fluted, sliced, cut into strips or diced. Tiny pickled gherkins are another good salad add-in.

Garlic.   According to Moslem legend, when Satan stepped out of the Garden of Eden after the fall of Man, garlic sprang up from the spot where he placed his left foot (and onions from where his right foot touched). It may be devilish but it's indispensable for salad makers. Keep it on hand in several forms. Fresh garlic is stronger than powdered. You can make your own garlic salt by combining 3 parts of salt or salt substitute with 1 part of garlic granules, flakes or powder. Garlic is also sold as a ready-to-use juice.

To use fresh garlic, break off a clove from the head, dip it in hot water to loosen skin, peel, then chop or mince or mash in garlic press before adding to salad or dressing. Its flavor can also be added more subtly to salads either by rubbing the inside of the empty salad bowl with halved garlic or adding slivers to salad oil or dressing to "flavorize" it before the greens are dressed. Remember, less is more. Salad with too much garlic can sometimes ruin what's to come. If you're planning to follow your salad with a delicate dessert, use the mild-flavored gourmet garlic called elephant garlic, or switch to shallots.

Ginger Root.   Peeled and sliced, shredded or grated, fresh ginger adds an interesting flavor and aroma to salads. Peel and chop the root and store in a small jar of sherry. Small pieces may "juiced" straight into the salad bowl with a garlic press.

Jerusalem Artichokes.   No relation to Jerusalem or to the green globe artichokes, their name is derived from Italian *girasole*, sunflower. The Jerusalem artichoke plant is really a 6- to 12-foot relative of the sunflower. Sunchokes, as they are also known, have been cultivated for centuries and were a common fixture in Cape Cod salads in the 1600s.

The edible parts are the underground tubers, which look somewhat like ginger root or small knobby potatoes. The flesh is white, sweet and crisp, rather like water chestnuts. Look for firm tubers, heavy for their size, with clean skins that are free from mold. Good raw and thinly sliced or steamed. They keep one week refrigerated. Peel just before using and drop in acidulated water to prevent browning or discoloration.

Leeks.   These look like giant scallions but their flavor is gentler. In France, the leek is considered the poor man's asparagus. Choose small–to medium-sized leeks and use them raw or blanch and chill and use in place of other types of onions.

Mushrooms. The bland, light tan or white cultivated mushrooms may be sliced, diced or minced raw for any mixed salads. One small mushroom has less than 3 calories. Wipe clean before using (never soak). Buy only what you can use in a week, and store refrigerated in a paper bag.

Peas. Buy tiny frozen peas, thaw, and use uncooked to put a nutlike crunch into any vegetable salad. Lightly steamed fresh sugar peas and snow peas may be eaten pods and all.

Pepper. Sweet-fleshed peppers come in various sizes and shapes and range in color from green to yellow and red. Sweet peppers may be used as salad vegetables cooked or raw, for pickling in brine or chopped as a dressing ingredient. A good salad source of vitamins A and C. Less than 7 calories an ounce. And no, they are not related to any of the peppercorns.

Refrigerate unwashed raw peppers in the crisper. To peel a pepper, place it directly over a burner of a gas or electric stove turned on high heat. Roast, turning frequently, until the outer skin is black and blistered (5 to 10 minutes). Or, blacken under the broiler, also turning frequently. Drop peppers in the sink and peel under cold running water, slipping off the blistered skin. Slice open and remove seeds and membrane and dry on paper towels.

Pine Nuts. Pine nuts (also known as Indian nuts or by their Italian name, pignoli) are probably the most underutilized of all nuts. Price may be a deterrent, since they often sell for as much as $8 a pound. (Pass up those little bottles of imported pignoli: At $1.50 an ounce you're paying $24 a pound.) Labor costs are part of the reason. Nuts must be carefully extracted from their tight cones, then from their thin, thin shells. Although many are imported, pine nuts are also a native American food and the pine cones can be gathered freely in the forests of the Southwest.

Pine nuts should be bought in small quantities and stored carefully in a tightly closed jar in the refrigerator because they spoil quickly. Roasting them on a cookie sheet at 350° for 12 minutes or sautéing them in a small amount of butter or olive oil brings out their full flavor.

Pine nuts are exceptional when added to a mushroom/spinach/pasta salad. They're also good in homemade breads and crackers. (See Pesto Presto Salad Bread, page 154)

Scallions. Scallions (green onions) will keep refrigerated and unwashed in a plastic bag for one week. They are an inexpensive shallot substitute and their green parts may be used as a chive substitute.

Shallots. These are a mild and aromatic member of the onion family. They grow in clusters like garlic. Shallot flavor is complex, both oniony and garlic-like. Dry, firm round shallots are best stored in a cool, dry place. They'll keep one to two months. Use as you would garlic. If tiny green shoots appear, snip and use those in your salad, too. Shallots may be used in recipes that call for scallions.

Sprouts. Pale and tender soybean or Mung bean sprouts add a nonintrusive flavor and lots of crispness to salads. Alfalfa adds a grassy note; radish and sunflower sprouts provide a peppery taste; wheat sprouts are nutty; lentils, chickpea and pea sprouts add eye appeal, texture and nutrition.

Wash store-bought sprouts gently and refrigerate in plastic bags. Do not remove the vitamin-rich hulls and roots.

To grow your own sprouts, wash seeds, then soak them overnight in a quart jar of lukewarm water. The following morning, cover the mouth of the jar with netting or cheesecloth, secure with a rubber band, drain, rinse and drain the beans, then store the jar in a warm, dark cupboard. Rinse and drain two to four times a day for about three days. One-third cup of dry seeds will produce two to three cups of sprouts.

Whole Grains (millet, buckwheat, cracked wheat, brown rice). Cooked and chilled, these grains can be an important addition to either vegetable or fruit salads. They supply B vitamins, minerals, protein and average around 200 calories a cup.

Exotic Edibles

Asian pears. Small and light green, round, with the crispy texture of apples but the juicy taste of pears.

Cactus leaf (nopales). Paddle-shaped leaves of the prickly pear cactus, with a peppery flavor. Remove the thorns, chop and eat raw in salads, or try them on a salad of tomatoes and onions dressed with oil, vinegar and oregano.

Daikon. This Oriental turnip-like radish is spongy, pungent, low in calories and good shredded or grated in raw or pickled salads. If it's sold with blossoms, take them home, too. They're edible.

Edible Flowers. Chinese, Arabs, Greeks and Romans use peonies, daisies, lotus, roses, violets, carnations and other blossoms to flavor and beautify their salad bowls. Flowers even have health properties. Roses are not only red, they're rich in vitamins A (as are dandelion buds) and C. So are violets, which also add iron and a peppery flavor to salad bowls. Nasturtium leaves make a good watercress substitute, and nasturtium seeds are nature's own capers. Other edible buds for the salad bowl include: primroses, marigolds, day lilies and flowering squash blossoms.

Jícama. A large, turnip-shaped root vegetable with a thin, light-brown skin. It has a crisp white flesh, similar in texture to a radish or a potato, although the jícama is sweeter. Jícama is available in Latin American markets and in Oriental markets, where it is called yam bean. At only 5 calories a slice, it is good raw in any salad. May be used in place of potatoes, water chestnuts, bamboo shoots or white turnips.

Long Beans. Chinese string beans about sixteen inches long. Tougher than American types; blanch before using.

Maui and Vidalia Onions. Sweet and as crunchy as apples, low in calories.

Miniature Vegetables. You can find tiny artichokes, yellow zucchini, beets, scallopini squash, Japanese and Italian purple eggplants, round white eggplants and carrots. Cook them as you would larger varieties of the same vegetable, but reduce cooking time. Most can also be used raw, diced or grated.

Passion fruit. Egg-size, with purplish-brown skin that is wrinkled when ripe and is eaten raw. Slice and use seeds and all.

Prickly pear. Remove the stickers from this cactus fruit and use steamed or raw in fruit salads. Taste is similar to watermelon.

Salsify. A long black root with an oysterish flavor (also called oyster plant). Peel and grate into salads.

Tamarillo. A New Zealand tree tomato that's very tart, filled with seeds. Mix with sweeter fruits, such as bananas.

Tropical Fruits. Peel and use raw for low-calorie salads; they supply more vitamins A and C and calcium than common fruits. Try kiwis, papayas, mangos and cherimoyas (which taste like vanilla sherbet).

HOW LONG WILL IT KEEP?

Don't count on more than a week for anything other than carrots or radishes. And potatoes? They take the "keepers" sweepstakes. Stored in a dark, ventilated pantry, they're good for months.

PROTEIN BOOSTERS FOR THE WHOLE MEAL SALAD BOWL

If a salad is your whole meal, you have to make sure it contains enough protein. The most obvious sources are meat, fish and poultry. But even if you are a vegetarian your salad bowl can contain all the protein you need from one meal—12 to 19 grams.

MEAT, FISH AND POULTRY SUBSTITUTES

The most common non-meat protein of all is cheese: 1 to 2 ounces can turn a salad into a meal. In addition to protein, cheese adds B vitamins and if it's garlic-flavored or Liederkranz, even aroma to a centerpiece salad. Cheese is a good no-cook alternative to meat and poultry. And the right cheese strips instead of sirloin strips can save you cash and calories.

Cheese adds protein, calcium, zinc and vitamins B and A. But buy the real thing. Processed cheeses may be reduced in fat or cholesterol-free, but they are usually rich in artificial color and other additives, and you won't necessarily save on sodium and/or calories.

How can you tell the difference? Read the label. The first ingredient of real cheese is milk or cheese, not water or caseinates. Real cheese doesn't contain vegetable oil or casein, a milk protein used in imitation cheeses. It also doesn't contain gums and cellulose added to produce thickness (bulk) that processing destroys.

• A good way to reduce cheese calories is to switch to part-skim-milk cheeses. Skim-milk cheeses are lower in calories and fat but higher in sodium.

• Three cheeses with reduced fat: sapsago (a skim-milk Parmesan and Romano substitute), hoop cheese and farmer's cheese (a cottage/cream cheese alternative).

• You can also make your own protein boosters for salads. All of the following may be frozen after shaping or after cooking. When ready to use, serve at room temperature (or chilled in salads that are tastier cold).

TWO TIPS

MIXTURE 1:

    1 cup cooked, drained barley
    1 cup slightly crushed cooked chick-peas
    ½ cup cooked oatmeal
    ¼ teaspoon salt or substitute
    1 teaspoon paprika
    2 tablespoons soy sauce
      Ground black pepper, to taste

MIXTURE 2:

    1 small stalk celery
    ½ small onion
    1 scallion
    1 clove garlic, peeled

Homemade Vegetable Protein #1
(bean/grain)

• Preheat oven to 325°.
• Combine Mixture 1 in a bowl.
• In a blender or food processor, chop Mixture 2.
• Add mixture 2 to Mixture 1. Combine well.
• Shape into patties, "sausages" or "meatballs" and chill. Bake at 325° on a greased cookie sheet for 20 minutes. Cool before serving.

Makes 12 salad servings. Leftovers may be frozen.

Variation: To make "meat loaf," press the combined ingredients into a greased loaf pan and bake for 30 minutes in a preheated 325° oven; other grains such as rice or cracked wheat can be substituted for the barley; navy, pinto or other beans can be substituted for chick-peas. Nuts and seeds can also be added.

Homemade Vegetable Protein #2
(double nut)

1 cup finely chopped pecans
1 cup finely chopped walnuts
1 cup fresh bread crumbs
1 cup chopped, seeded, peeled tomatoes
¼ cup milk, beaten with 2 eggs
½ cup finely chopped onion
¼ cup minced parsley
½ teaspoon crumbled fresh or ¼ teaspoon dried sage leaves
¼ teaspoon paprika
½ teaspoon salt or substitute
Freshly ground pepper to taste

• Combine all ingredients. Form into desired shapes. Chill until ready to use.
• Cook as directed in Homemade Vegetable Protein #1.

Makes 4 cups.

Variations: Use peanuts, almonds or cashews in place of walnuts or pecans.

5-Minute Meatballs: Shape either of the above mixtures into tiny meatballs. Sauté 5 minutes in oil in a hot skillet. Cool and use in salads.

SALAD DAYS AND NIGHTS

VEGETARIAN SALADS

2 cups Boston or Bibb lettuce leaves
1 cucumber
1 cup olive oil
⅓ cup white wine vinegar
½ teaspoon salt or substitute
¼ teaspoon freshly ground pepper
½ cup finely chopped purple basil (use green if purple is unavailable)
1 cup cubed Homemade Vegetable Protein (page 35, 36)
2 3-ounce individual French or domestic goat cheeses
Olive oil
Basil sprigs for garnish

CHÈVRE SALAD WITH CUCUMBER AND PURPLE BASIL

• Arrange lettuce on 2 salad plates.
• Wash and dry the cucumber. Score the sides vertically with the tines of a fork. Cut into ⅛-inch-thick slices and arrange in two concentric circles of overlapping slices on the 2 salad plates. Cover with plastic wrap and chill until serving time.
• Combine olive oil, vinegar, salt or substitute, pepper and chopped basil. Stir in Homemade Vegetable Protein. Set aside.
• Just before serving, place goat cheeses in a shallow baking dish and dot with a little oil. Bake in a preheated 450° oven for 5 minutes. Cool slightly. Place on top of cucumbers and lettuce.
• Beat dressing ingredients well, spoon over cheese, cucumbers and lettuce; serve while chèvre is still warm, garnished with basil sprigs.

2 servings.

Serve with: Nutty Mix (page 148), Super Salad Croissants (page 159) or assorted whole-grain wafers.

Variations: Substitute 1 cup shredded cabbage and 1 cup torn fresh spinach leaves for the lettuce; substitute crumbled Cheddar for goat cheese; substitute cold cuts (rare roast beef, baked ham, prosciutto) for the cheese.

FRUIT AND FIBER SALAD

4 cups fresh spinach leaves
1 quart fresh strawberries
1 cup any soft sweet cheese such as ricotta, Neufchâtel or cream cheese, crumbled

SWEET-SOUR DRESSING:

½ cup olive oil
1½ to 2 tablespoons strawberry vinegar (or substitute red wine vinegar plus ¼ teaspoon sugar)
1 tablespoon yogurt
Salt or substitute and freshly ground pepper, to taste

• Choose spinach with small leaves. Remove stems, wash and dry well. Wash berries and remove stems. Leave berries whole or cut in half. Combine greens, berries and cheese, tossing gently.
• Combine dressing ingredients; adjust sweetness or tartness to taste. Pour over fruit, cheese and greens.

3–4 servings.

Serve with: Homemade Raisins (page 147), or top with Salad Sprinkles (page 131) of your choice.

Variations: Substitute blueberries, blackberries or cherries for the strawberries; use radicchio or New Zealand spinach in place of spinach; use Sunflower Dressing (page 131) in place of the Sweet-Sour.

4-STAR 3-GREEN SUPERBOWL

Lemon Vinaigrette (see recipe next page)
1 head Bibb lettuce, torn into bite-sized pieces
2 bunches watercress, stemmed
2 large Belgian endives, cored and cut lengthwise into ¼-inch strips
6 to 8 green unscented geranium leaves, cut into very thin strips (optional)
1½ cups Homemade Vegetable Protein (pages 35, 36)
¼ cup minced fresh parsley or chives
¾ cup grated Parmesan or Romano cheese
Whole unscented geranium leaves (optional)

• Prepare Lemon Vinaigrette and set aside.
• Combine lettuce, watercress, endives and sliced geranium leaves in salad bowl. Add Homemade Vegetable Protein. Pour dressing over greens, and sprinkle with parsley and grated cheese. Toss well. Garnish with whole geranium leaves if desired. Serve immediately.

4 servings.

1 small clove garlic
1½ teaspoons salt or substitute
½ teaspoon Dijon-style mustard
2 to 3 tablespoons fresh lemon juice
⅓ cup olive oil
1 teaspoon red wine vinegar
  Freshly ground pepper, to taste

Lemon Vinaigrette

• Combine garlic and salt in small bowl or mortar; mash until pasty. Work in mustard and lemon juice.
• Transfer to medium bowl. Gradually whisk in oil. Add vinegar and pepper to taste.

Serve with: Olive Caviar (page 159, omit toasts) on Herb Wheels (page 152) or sesame breadsticks with a cheese dip.

Variations: If you pass up the peppery geranium leaves, add an extra ½ teaspoon freshly ground pepper; use shallots in place of garlic. Other greens to substitute: collards, turnip greens, kale. For a nonvegetarian version, substitute fresh or canned crabmeat, salmon or shrimp for the Homemade Vegetable Protein.

1 small head of a soft lettuce such as Boston or Bibb
1 cup fresh violet leaves
½ cup alfalfa sprouts or ½ cup cubed cooked zucchini
⅔ cup tofu strips or 5-Minute Meatballs (page 36)
  Violet flowers for garnish

BLUE-EYED SALAD FOR SPRING GARDENERS

• Wash lettuce and violet leaves quickly under cold running water. Tear leaves into bite-sized pieces, add sprouts and tofu strips and mix. Sprinkle flowers on top. Dress with the vinaigrette of your choice.

2 servings.

Serve with: Fruit-Filled Croissants (page 160) or fresh raw peas in the pod.

Variations: Use the leaves and buds of another edible flower such as geraniums or dandelions in place of violets; use sliced blue or purple grapes in place of violets; for nonvegetarian version, use slivered baked ham in place of tofu.

SEAWEED SALAD

SEASONINGS:

    2 teaspoons soy sauce
    1 teaspoon honey or 1 teaspoon sugar
  ⅔ cup water
    Pinch of salt or salt substitute

GREENS:

  ½ head medium cabbage, shredded
    5 cups boiling water plus ½ teaspoon salt
    2 tablespoons oil
    3 cakes tofu, diced
  ⅔ cup dried arame seaweed, freshened in water and drained*

DRESSING:

  ¼ cup nut butter, such as peanut, almond or sunflower seed
    2 tablespoons honey or 1 tablespoon sugar
 1½ tablespoons soy sauce

• Combine seasoning mixture and set aside. Drop cabbage into boiling salted water, return to a boil and cook 30 seconds; remove pan from heat. Drain cabbage in a colander.
• Heat oil in a skillet and lightly stir-fry the tofu with the arame. Add seasoning mixture and cabbage. Bring to a boil, then reduce heat and simmer, covered, until cabbage is soft (about 10 minutes).
• While tofu and vegetables are simmering, combine dressing ingredients. Thin to desired consistency with small amounts of water and soy sauce. Stir dressing into vegetables just before serving.

2–3 servings.

Serve with: Assorted whole-grain wafers and carrot curls or plain bread and Fancy Butter (page 155).

Variations: Substitute Chinese cabbage for regular cabbage; garnish with edible fresh flowers (dandelion buds, carnations or nasturtiums); use string cheese pulled into strands in place of seaweed. For a nonvegetarian version, substitute ⅔ cup seafood such as baby shrimp or sliced scallops for the tofu.

---

*If you like linguini, you'll like arame, a spaghetti-like seaweed vegetable. A good second choice: pasta-like hijicki.

2 pounds eggplant, trimmed, peeled and cut into
    one-inch cubes
Juice of one lemon
3 hard-boiled eggs, sliced or diced
⅓ cup snipped fresh dill
⅓ cup chopped scallions
⅓ cup olive oil
¼ cup lemon juice
2 cups homemade yogurt cheese*
Salt or substitute
Freshly ground black pepper
2 to 3 cups fresh spinach leaves

*EGGPLANT
SALAD WITH
EGGS*

• In saucepan, cook eggplant with juice of lemon in boiling salted water for 10 minutes. Drain.
• Combine eggplant, eggs, dill, scallions, olive oil and lemon juice. Fold in yogurt and salt (or substitute) and pepper to taste.
• Serve over spinach leaves.

3–4 servings.

Serve with: Super Salad Croissants (page 159) or assorted Melba toasts.

Variations: Substitute 1 cup fresh mustard greens or corn salad greens for 1 cup spinach; use diced tofu in place of eggs.

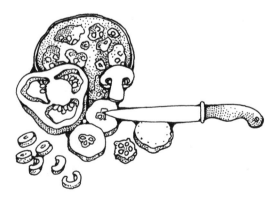

*To make yogurt cheese, line a sieve with a double thickness of cheesecloth and pour in 1 pint of plain yogurt. Cover and let drain over a bowl at least 2 hours or as long as overnight.

LETTUCE HEARTS SALAD WITH MELTED BUTTER

3 to 4 very fresh lettuce hearts (Boston, romaine or butterhead)
3 to 4 tablespoons clarified sweet butter, at room temperature
2 tablespoons lemon juice
1 tablespoon lime juice
1 clove garlic, minced
  Crushed dried rosemary, to taste
  Dill, to taste
1 cup Homemade Vegetable Protein (pages 35, 36)
  Freshly ground black pepper

• Separate lettuce leaves. Wash carefully, dry and chill.
• Combine clarified butter, lemon and lime juices, garlic, rosemary and dill. Add Homemade Vegetable Protein to butter sauce and mix well.
• Pour quickly over the lettuce and toss until leaves glisten. Top with plenty of fresh ground pepper and serve at once.

2 servings.

Serve with: A side dish of Exotic Edibles (page 32) cubed or slivered, on the side.

Variation: Serve with Super Salad Croissants (pages 35, 36) and omit Homemade Vegetable Protein.

2 scallions with tops, trimmed
2 pounds celery hearts, trimmed
1 tablespoon Sichuan or white peppercorns
¼ cup soy sauce
2 tablespoons sesame oil
1 tablespoon rice vinegar
1 tablespoon peeled, minced, fresh ginger
2 teaspoons sugar (optional)
1 cup 5-Minute Meatballs (page 36)
2½ cups any lettuce or cabbage, shredded

HEARTS OF THE EAST

• Mince scallions, setting 1 tablespoon of tops aside for garnish. Combine the remaining tops with white part and set aside (about 2 tablespoons).

• Cut each celery heart in half crosswise, then cut each half lengthwise into slices about ¼-inch thick. Heat a large heavy saucepan of water over high heat to boiling, blanch celery 30 seconds. Drain in colander, refresh under cold running water, then drain and pat dry with paper towels. Transfer to a large bowl.

• Heat a small heavy skillet over medium heat until hot. Add peppercorns; heat, stirring constantly, until fragrant (about 2 minutes). Remove from heat; transfer peppercorns to blender or food processor. Blend to a powder.

• Combine ground peppercorns, soy sauce, sesame oil, the 2 tablespoons minced whole scallions, vinegar, ginger and sugar in a small bowl; stir until sugar is dissolved. Pour mixture over celery. Add the meatballs and toss to coat.

• Transfer to serving platter layered with the shredded lettuce or cabbage. Sprinkle with reserved scallion tops. Serve immediately, while still warm.

3 servings.

Serve with: Puffy shrimp chips (sold in the Oriental food section of supermarkets) on the side or Nasturtium Bugles (page 149) on top.

Variations: Substitute sliced celery root for celery hearts or use water chestnuts; substitute ¾ teaspoon ginger juice for the minced ginger.

*KIMCHI SALAD ON THE QUICK**

3 cups Chinese cabbage, trimmed
1 cup Homemade Vegetable Protein (pages 35, 36)
2 garlic cloves, mashed
1 teaspoon hot pepper sauce or crushed red pepper flakes
1 to 2 tablespoons soy sauce
1 teaspoon vinegar
1 teaspoon salt or substitute
1 tablespoon sugar or 1 teaspoon honey
1½ cups soft leafy greens such as Boston or Oak Tip lettuce

• Chop cabbage into 1½-inch pieces and combine with all the other ingredients except lettuce. Mix well.
• Taste and adjust the flavor with more red pepper, soy sauce and vinegar, as desired. Cover and let stand at room temperature for 1 hour. Serve over greens.

2 servings.

Serve with: Toasted sesame seeds or walnuts or Fake Bacon Bits (page 147) on top.

Variations: For a nonvegetarian kimchi, skip the Homemade Vegetable Protein and substitute 1 cup cold diced turkey or chicken and garnish with crumbled bits of bacon.

*Kimchi is a national Korean relish, rather like garlicky and peppery sauerkraut. Usually hot-tasting and time-consuming to prepare, here's proof it can be fast and still flavorful.

2 14-ounce cans hearts of palm
3 cups any mixed greens
1 cup broiled or baked and chilled soybean tempeh,*
   in cubes or strips
½ pound fresh mushrooms
20 red or yellow cherry tomatoes, halved
1 small red onion, peeled and sliced into thin rings
1 small clove garlic, finely minced
¼ cup lime or lemon juice
½ cup olive oil
¼ cup finely chopped parsley
   Salt or substitute
   Freshly ground pepper

HEARTS OF PALM SALAD PLUS

• Drain the hearts of palm. Cut the pieces into ¾-inch rounds. Place them in a salad bowl with torn greens and tempeh.
• Thinly slice the mushrooms and add them. Add the tomatoes, onion rings, garlic, lime juice, olive oil, parsley, salt or substitute and pepper to taste. Toss, adding more olive oil if desired.

4 servings.

Serve with: Salad Crackerjacks (page 147) or a do-it-yourself gourmet mix. Try 1 cup of costly macadamia nuts mixed with 1 cup of economical roasted peanuts or soy nuts.

Variations: Substitute 1½ cups of diced or slivered turkey for tempeh; use basil or watercress in place of parsley; omit lemon or lime juice and oil and dress with Low-Calorie Grapefruit Vinaigrette (page 130).

*Available frozen at health food stores.

LETTUCE-FREE SALAD #1
(with mint)

2 10-ounce packages frozen tiny new peas (*petits pois*)* thawed at room temperature
3 medium carrots, pared and coarsely shredded (about 2 cups)
⅔ cup thinly sliced scallions with tops
1¼ cups diced raw or cooked and chilled tofu
½ cup finely chopped fresh parsley
¼ cup finely chopped fresh mint leaves
½ cup olive oil (a strong-flavored oil is best here)
2 tablespoons red wine vinegar
1 teaspoon salt or substitute
½ teaspoon freshly ground pepper
Fresh mint sprigs

• Combine peas, carrots, scallions, tofu, parsley and chopped mint in a large bowl. Refrigerate, covered, until ready to serve.
• Whisk together oil, vinegar, salt and pepper in small bowl. Just before serving, pour over salad; toss to combine. Garnish with mint sprigs and serve.

4 servings.

Serve with: Salad Doodles (page 147) or fresh alfalfa sprouts.

Variation: Use garlic shoots (the chive-flavored greens that sprout from over-the-hill garlic; place in water to grow shoots) in place of scallions.

Petits pois are an incredible edible uncooked. Thaw only to add crunch to salads.

2 large seedless cucumbers, unpared, rinsed, thinly
  sliced
1 medium onion, thinly sliced
¼ cup cider vinegar
2 tablespoons water
1 teaspoon sugar or ½ teaspoon honey
1 teaspoon salt or substitute
½ teaspoon freshly ground pepper
2 cups 5-Minute Meatballs (page 36)

LETTUCE-FREE SALAD #2 *(with onion)*

• Toss cucumbers and onion in large bowl; add vinegar, water, sugar, salt and pepper.
• Add meatballs. Refrigerate, covered, 2 to 3 hours. Before serving, drain off marinade; reserve for storing leftover salad.

4 servings.

Serve with: Roasted Almonds (page 149) or toasted rye wafers.

Variations: If seedless cucumbers are not available, substitute 4 regular unwaxed cucumbers, seeded; substitute shallots for onion.

DOUBLE ARTICHOKE SALAD

⅓ cup olive oil
1 to 2 cloves garlic, slivered
1 large head romaine lettuce, leaves separated, rinsed and dried
12 ounces raw Jerusalem artichokes, pared and thinly sliced (about 2 cups)
1 cup fresh cooked, canned, or thawed frozen artichoke hearts
3 tablespoons fresh lemon juice
3 tablespoons minced parsley
½ tablespoon salt or substitute
Freshly ground pepper, to taste
2 medium tomatoes, peeled and cut into wedges
1 small green pepper, seeded and cut into ¼-inch slices
⅓ cup freshly grated Parmesan cheese
1 cup julienned Jarlsberg cheese

• Place oil and garlic in a large bowl and let stand at room temperature 1 hour, then remove garlic and discard.
• Trim thick ends from romaine leaves and tear into bite-sized pieces, discarding tough stalks. Place in salad bowl with garlic-flavored oil and toss lightly. Add both kinds of artichokes, lemon juice, parsley, salt and pepper; toss well. Add tomatoes, green pepper and Parmesan cheese; toss gently to combine. Top with Jarlsberg strips or Egg White Croutons (page 145).

4 servings.

Serve with: Garlic-buttered matzos or Cool Cucumber Wafers (page 155).

Variations: Substitute endive for romaine; use water chestnuts in place of Jerusalem artichokes; use fresh watercress, mint or summer savory in place of parsley; substitute low-sodium Swiss cheese for Jarlsberg.

⅓ cup olive oil
2 tablespoons fresh lemon juice
2 tablespoons grated onion
1 clove garlic, mashed, or ½ teaspoon minced
    shallots
1 medium tomato, peeled, seeded and chopped
¼ cup minced parsley
   Salt or substitute, to taste
   Freshly ground pepper, to taste
1 cup Homemade Vegetable Protein (pages 35, 36)
2 to 3 cups drained cooked soybeans
2 cups any lettuce, torn or shredded

SIMPLE SOYBEAN SALAD

• Combine all the ingredients except soybeans and lettuce. Mix well. Add soybeans and toss. Chill before serving over the greens.

2–3 servings.

Serve with: Small buttered biscuits, Homemade Hardtack (page 151) or canned onion rings (heat to crisp before serving).

Variations: Substitute cooked kidney beans, chick-peas or pinto beans for soybeans; use alfalfa or bean sprouts in place of parsley; substitute 1 cup coarsely grated low-fat mozzarella for the Homemade Vegetable Protein; try canned pimiento in place of raw tomato.

WHITE BEAN SALAD

1½ cups dried white beans, soaked overnight in water to cover
2 carrots, chopped
1 onion, chopped
  Bouquet garni (tarragon, thyme, dillweed, marjoram, oregano, sage, savory, rosemary)
½ cup minced parsley
½ cup extra-virgin olive oil (preferably green Tuscan)
2 tablespoons lemon juice
3 scallions, including green part, chopped, or 1 leek
  Salt or substitute, to taste
  Freshly ground pepper, to taste
1½ cups torn spinach
1½ cups torn arugula
1 cup ricotta cheese
  Fresh parsley, tarragon or summer savory to garnish

• Bring beans and soaking liquid to a boil with carrots, onion, bouquet garni and parsley. Simmer 60 to 90 minutes, until beans are tender but not mushy.
• Prepare dressing: combine oil, lemon juice, scallions, salt and pepper.
• Drain beans and spoon into a bowl. Add dressing, toss and let marinate at room temperature 1 to 2 hours. Arrange the greens on individual serving plates, spoon on the beans and top each with a fourth of the ricotta. Sprinkle with garnishing herbs.

4 servings.

Serve with: Roasted Almonds (page 149) on the side.

Variations: For a more robust dressing, use red wine vinegar, anchovies and garlic mashed to a paste instead of the lemon juice and scallions; substitute cottage cheese or pot cheese for ricotta.

Hint: Save leftover beans to make a white bean salad spread: Mix beans with olive oil and fresh mint leaves and puree in a food processor or blender. Serve on toasted crackers.

1½   cups fresh dandelion greens
1½   cups fresh spinach
 2   tablespoons fresh lemon juice or cider vinegar
 2   hard-boiled eggs, sliced
½   cup cooked dried beans (pinto, soy, etc.), chilled

PECAN DRESSING:

½   cup ground pecans
1¼   cups vegetable oil
 3   tablespoons lemon juice plus 2 tablespoons cider
     vinegar
¼   teaspoon cayenne pepper plus 1 clove garlic,
     chopped

SPRING SALAD WITH PECAN DRESSING

• Combine all dressing ingredients, shake well and set aside.
• Lay the greens in ice water and lemon juice or vinegar for 1 hour. Remove, drain well. Dry with paper towels.
• Tear the greens into bite-sized pieces and place in a chilled bowl. When ready to serve, toss with dressing and garnish with slices of hard-boiled eggs and cooked chilled beans.

3 servings.

Serve with: Homemade Chinese Breadsticks (page 154), Chinese Chips (page 148) or sprinkle with toasted chow mein noodles from the can.

Variations: Substitute Basic Fresh Fruit Vinegar (page 174) of your choice for Pecan Dressing. Use arugula in place of dandelion; Bibb in place of spinach.

JÍCAMA-ORANGE SALAD

1 medium jícama (about 1 pound) (see Glossary)
3 large oranges
1 medium red onion, thinly sliced
1½ cups tofu strips
1 cup fresh orange juice
¼ cup fresh lime juice
1 tablespoon finely chopped fresh coriander
2 teaspoons sugar or 1 teaspoon honey
1 teaspoon salt or substitute
1 lime, thinly sliced
Fresh mint, basil or parsley sprigs to garnish
2½ cups shredded Chinese cabbage
Salad Sprinkles (your choice, optional, page 150)

• Pare the jícama, then cut into thin strips (about 3 cups). Remove and discard peel and pith from oranges. Remove membranes, section, catching juice in a bowl, and combine with tofu strips and cabbage.
• Gently toss together with remaining ingredients except lime slices and garnish. Refrigerate 30 minutes.
• Top with sliced lime, mint and a Salad Sprinkle of your choice.

4 servings.

Serve with: Toasted dry-roasted nuts and pretzel sticks or Roasted Almonds (page 149).

Variations: Use spearmint vinegar in place of lime juice or substitute Lime Vinaigrette (page 130) for the dressing ingredients; use water chestnuts or radishes in place of jícama, or grapefruit instead of oranges.

1 bunch arugula
1 small head radicchio
1 egg yolk
½ teaspoon prepared mustard
3 tablespoons olive oil
½ clove garlic, pressed
   Coarse salt or substitute and freshly ground pepper
     to taste
2 teaspoons cider or fruit-flavored vinegar
1 tablespoon heavy cream or plain yogurt
2 tablespoons crumbled Gorgonzola cheese
1 tablespoon chopped walnuts
½ cup fresh raspberries
¼ cup bacon bits (optional)

ARUGULA RADICCHIO SUPERBOWL

• Trim the roots and stalks from the arugula and wash well. Clean radicchio leaves, pat dry with paper towels and chill.
• In a large bowl beat egg yolk and whisk in the mustard. Add the olive oil drop by drop, beating constantly until thick and creamy. Add the garlic and vinegar, then heavy cream, cheese, nuts and berries. Chill.
• When ready to serve, place greens in large salad bowl, toss the combined ingredients. Top with bacon bits if desired.

2 servings.

Serve with: Super Salad Croissants (page 159) or Swedish rye crackers on the side.

Variations: Use dandelion or turnip greens in place of arugula; 1 cup radish sprouts or grated radish instead of radicchio; substitute fresh blueberries or blackberries for raspberries.

SIZZLING CHEESE SALAD

4 cups torn mixed greens
¼ cup pitted ripe olives
6 whole sun-dried tomatoes or 6 fresh tomato wedges
¼ cup salad oil
¼ cup tarragon vinegar
2 teaspoons finely chopped scallion
1 teaspoon Dijon-style mustard
1 teaspoon nut oil (sesame, walnut, sunflower)
1 egg
1 tablespoon water
2 tablespoons cornmeal
1 tablespoon fine dry bread crumbs
1 tablespoon sesame seeds, toasted
2 teaspoons grated Parmesan cheese
4 ounces Neufchâtel cheese
1 cup shredded cheese of your choice (4 ounces)
2 tablespoons butter, melted
6 pita bread rounds, split and toasted

• On a serving platter, arrange greens, olives and tomatoes. Cover, chill.

• In screw-top jar combine salad oil, vinegar, scallion, mustard and nut oil. Cover and shake well. Chill until ready to use.

• In small bowl combine egg and water and set aside. In shallow bowl combine cornmeal, crumbs, sesame seeds and Parmesan and set aside.

• Beat the Neufchâtel and shredded cheese with an electric mixer until combined. Shape into 1-inch balls, flatten to form patties, dip first into egg mixture, then coat with the cornmeal mixture and put on a plate. Cover and chill until set.

• To fry patties: In a skillet, heat butter. Add patties and cook over medium-high heat about 10 minutes until golden, turning once.

• Shake dressing; drizzle over chilled salad. Arrange hot cheese patties and toasted pita on top.

4 servings.

Serve with: Julienned raw carrot or winter squash on the side.

Variations: Substitute green pepper rings for tomato wedges; substitute room-temperature cream cheese for Neufchâtel; use sesame crackers in place of pita.

VEGETABLE VEGETARIAN SALAD

2 large red or green bell peppers
1 tablespoon olive or other salad oil
2 scallions, including green parts, cut into ½-inch pieces
1 clove garlic, minced
1 medium zucchini or yellow summer squash, julienned
4 tablespoons red wine vinegar
½ teaspoon freshly ground pepper
3 to 4 cups spinach, washed, stemmed and torn
1 cup watercress
¾ cup crumbled feta cheese

• Roast peppers, whole, under broiler or over flame until skin is charred on all sides. Place in a brown paper bag, close bag and let stand 10 minutes to allow steam to loosen skins. Peel off skins; cut peppers in half. Remove seeds and veins, chop into 1-inch pieces and set aside.
• In a large skillet heat oil; add scallions, garlic and squash. Cook, stirring, over medium-high heat for 3 minutes. Add vinegar, ground pepper and spinach. Stir and toss mixture with 2 large spoons to coat spinach leaves. Add watercress and reserved bell peppers; toss one minute more.
• Remove from heat. Transfer salad mixture to a large serving bowl and sprinkle with cheese. Best served warm.

4–5 servings.

Serve with: Salt-free ruffled potato chips or Corn Diggers (page 149) on the side.

Variations: Substitute New Zealand spinach for spinach; use fresh sorrel or basil in place of watercress; use mild cheddar or goat cheese in place of feta; and if you're lucky enough to find unwaxed bell peppers and feel lazy, don't bother roasting them.

SPICY ORANGE AND OLIVE SALAD

3 large seedless oranges
⅛ teaspoon cayenne
1 teaspoon paprika
½ teaspoon crushed garlic
3 tablespoons olive oil
1 tablespoon vinegar
  Salt or substitute, to taste
  Freshly ground pepper, to taste
½ cup minced fresh parsley
12 pitted black olives (preferably imported Greek or Italian)
2 large hard-boiled eggs, diced
1½ cups dark greens (spinach, chard, arugula, rabe, turnip greens, etc.)

• Peel oranges, paring away all the white pith. Separate segments and cut into 1-inch pieces. Set aside.
• Place the cayenne, paprika, garlic, olive oil and vinegar in a large salad bowl, blend well with a wire whisk, then whisk in the salt and pepper.
• Add the orange pieces, parsley, olives and diced eggs. Toss gently to blend and serve cold or at room temperature over the greens.

2 servings.

Serve with: Toasted Grape-nuts or oyster crackers as a topping or garlic bread on the side.

Variations: Prepare the oranges, olives, eggs and greens as directed but dress with 30-Second Russian Dressing (page 120) or Hurry-Up Thousand Island (page 120); substitute an alternate citrus fruit, such as tangerines or tangelos.

2 tablespoons tarragon vinegar
1 teaspoon Dijon-style mustard
1 teaspoon anchovy paste or miso*
2 cloves garlic, crushed
3 tablespoons olive oil
3 tablespoons salad oil
4 cups sliced or shredded red radishes
1 cup shredded radicchio
1 cup cubed Swiss or Muenster cheese or 1 cup
    Homemade Vegetable Protein (pages 35, 36)
    Caraway seeds

DOUBLE RADISH SALAD

• In small jar with tight-fitting lid combine vinegar, mustard, anchovy paste and garlic. Cover and shake well. Add oils, cover and shake again. Set aside.
• In medium bowl combine radishes, radicchio and cheese. Pour on dressing and toss. Sprinkle with caraway seeds. Serve warm or cover and refrigerate.

4–5 servings.

Serve with: Whole Wheat Wafers (page 156) or toasted oyster crackers.

Variations: Substitute 1 cup of romaine or oak tip lettuce for the radicchio; substitute white (icicle) radishes for the red or use 2 cups of each; use Basic Salad Mustard (page 172) in place of Dijon-style mustard.

*Miso is a seasoning paste made from fermented soybeans. It can be found in many Oriental markets and health food stores.

NATURE'S BOWL #1

2½ cups mixed greens of your choice (try a combination of light and dark, such as escarole with spinach)

2 cups cooked dried chick-peas or one 16-ounce can, rinsed, drained and chilled

½ pound small potatoes, cooked and chilled

½ pound yellow or green snap beans, cooked and chilled

1 pound asparagus, trimmed, steamed and chilled

4 hard-boiled eggs, sliced

2 firm tomatoes, quartered

6 tablespoons low fat yogurt

3 tablespoons mayonnaise

3 large cloves garlic, minced

1 to 2 tablespoons Olive Caviar (page 159) or chopped black oil-cured olives

• Arrange mixed greens on a large serving platter.
• Mound chick-peas in the center. Group potatoes, beans and asparagus around them and arrange eggs and tomatoes around edge.
• In a small bowl, combine the yogurt, mayonnaise, garlic and olives. Let diners serve themselves.

2–3 servings.

Serve with: Super Salad Croissants (page 159), or pass vegetable sticks and unsalted nuts.

Variations: Substitute real red or black caviar for the Olive Caviar; use another legume such as canned French flageolets or Italian cannelini in place of chick-peas.

2 heads Bibb lettuce, separated into leaves
1 pink grapefruit, in sections
1 avocado, peeled and sliced lengthwise
3 to 4 cups cooked Homemade Vegetable Protein
   (pages 35, 36), slivered
¼ cup white wine vinegar
¾ cup olive oil
1½ teaspoons sugar (optional)
½ teaspoon paprika or dash of Tabasco
   Salt or substitute, to taste

NATURE'S BOWL #2

• Arrange lettuce on 4 individual salad plates.* Alternate pieces of grapefruit, avocado and Homemade Vegetable Protein on Bibb lettuce bed.
• Combine remaining ingredients and spoon over salads.

4 servings.

Serve with: Corn Chip Topping (page 145) on top or salt-free pretzels on the side.

Variations: Substitute Boston for Bibb lettuce; use white instead of pink grapefruit, or substitute navel orange sections or tangerines.

*Bibb salads are traditionally served on individual plates, but you can toss everything and serve from the bowl for a change of pace.

MIXED ROCKET POCKET SALAD

2 large potatoes
1 bunch arugula
1 bunch watercress, chopped
1 small head Boston lettuce or 2 heads Bibb lettuce
½ cup olive oil
2 tablespoons fresh lemon juice
  Salt or substitute, to taste
  Freshly ground pepper, to taste
1 cup 5-Minute Meatballs (page 136)
3 pita bread pockets

• Cook potatoes in their skins in boiling salted water (salt keeps them firm). While potatoes are cooking, trim the greens, discarding wilted leaves and cutting off stems. If leaves are big, tear in two. Tear lettuce into bite-sized pieces. Wash all greens, drain and pat or spin dry. Wrap in towels and refrigerate to crisp.

• Beat together oil and lemon juice until creamy, add salt and pepper. Drain cooked potatoes, peel and dice when cool enough to handle. Turn into a bowl, add 5-Minute Meatballs and toss with enough dressing to moisten. Add greens and adjust seasoning.

• Spoon into pita breads. Sprinkle with remaining dressing. Warm in a toaster oven before serving, if desired.

3 servings.

Serve with: Raw vegetable sticks.

Variations: Substitute romaine for the Boston lettuce; use radish sprouts in place of watercress. For a nonvegetarian version, substitute 1 cup cocktail-size meatballs for 5-Minute Meatballs. Try 1-2-3 Tahini (page 119) instead of the dressing given.

1½ cups whole wheat berries*
 1 clove garlic, crushed and finely chopped
 1 small bunch scallions including greens, peeled and
    chopped
   Juice of ½ lemon
 ¼ cup olive oil
 ½ pound feta cheese, crumbled
   Freshly ground pepper, to taste
2½ cups mixed greens

*WHEAT BERRY
SALAD*

• In a saucepan, combine wheat berries and 2 cups water.
Cook, partially covered, over medium heat until tender
but not mushy (15 to 20 minutes). Cool.
• Combine wheat berries with remaining ingredients except the greens and the pepper. Spoon over greens and
grind on pepper.

4 servings.

Serve with: Toasted oyster crackers as topping or Olive
Caviar Toasts (page 159) on the side.

Variations: Substitute lime juice for the lemon juice; substitute a mild goat cheese for the feta; use cooked brown
or wild rice in place of wheat berries.

*Wheat berries (for sprouting, too) are sold in health food stores or by mail.

SELF-DRESSING SALAD #1

1 pound bean sprouts
½ pound mushrooms, sliced
1 cup chopped raw Jerusalem artichokes
1 cup sliced cucumbers
1 tomato, sliced
3 scallions with tops, sliced
½ cup salad oil
2 tablespoons white wine vinegar
1 small clove garlic, crushed
¼ teaspoon oregano
¼ teaspoon salt or substitute
⅛ teaspoon freshly ground pepper
½ teaspoon dry mustard
2 cups mixed greens

• Arrange first six ingredients in shallow bowl. Place oil, vinegar and seasonings in blender and blend until smooth.
• Pour dressing over vegetables and toss. Cover and chill at least 1 hour. Spoon over greens and serve at once.

4 servings.

Serve with: Roaster's Choice Croutons (page 147) or Roasted Almonds (page 149).

Variations: Substitute water chestnuts or chilled, drained artichoke hearts for Jerusalem artichokes; use leeks in place of scallions.

2 pounds Jerusalem artichokes
2 teaspoons lemon juice or 1 teaspoon dried lemon peel
¼ cup finely chopped onion
1 teaspoon salt or substitute
⅛ teaspoon freshly ground pepper
½ cup chopped celery
¼ cup salad dressing of your choice
½ cup mayonnaise
2 hard-boiled eggs, sliced
2 cups mixed greens

SELF-DRESSING SALAD #2

• Scrub artichokes. Cut into bite-sized pieces. Place in saucepan in 1 inch salted boiling water.
• Add lemon juice, cover and cook 5 to 8 minutes, until tender-crisp when tested with a fork. Do not overcook. Drain and cool.
• Combine artichokes in bowl with onion, salt, pepper, celery and salad dressing. Cover and refrigerate 2 hours. Before serving, mix in mayonnaise and eggs and toss gently until well mixed. Serve over greens.

4 servings.

Serve with: Corn Chip Topping (page 145) or assorted sprouts.

Variation: Substitute a lemony-flavored herb such as lemon grass for lemon juice. Gardening lemon lovers love this lemon rind-flavored southeast Asian herb. Sold dried, powdered and fresh (see "Mail Order Sources").

VEGETARIAN ANTIPASTO

1 bunch fresh beets (about 8 medium), tops removed,
   or one 16-ounce can whole small beets, quartered
1 small head cauliflower, divided into flowerets
1 small bunch broccoli, divided into flowerets
2 cups arugula or radicchio torn in bite-sized pieces
1 cup cooked Homemade Vegetable Protein (pages
   35, 36) sliced
½ cup watercress, stems trimmed
½ cup olive or vegetable oil
¼ cup red wine vinegar
4 tablespoons Dijon-style mustard

• If using fresh beets, cook, covered, in rapidly boiling water until they can be pierced easily with a fork (25 to 30 minutes). Drain beets under cold running water. When cool enough to handle, slip off skins and quarter.
• Place cauliflower and broccoli in steamer over rapidly boiling water, cover and steam until tender, about 10 minutes. Refresh under cold running water, then drain.
• Arrange greens on platter. Arrange cauliflower, broccoli and Homemade Vegetable Protein in concentric circles on top. Garnish with beets and watercress. Combine oil, vinegar and mustard and pour over salad or serve on the side.

4 servings.

Serve with: Olive Caviar Toasts (page 159) or Melba toast and assorted olives.

Variations: Use romaine, chard or spinach in place of the Italian greens; substitute Walnut Vinaigrette (page 130) for the dressing given.

½ pound fusilli or other spiral pasta
2 medium red peppers, finely diced
2 medium yellow peppers, finely diced
1 medium red onion, finely chopped
1 cup toasted pine nuts (see Glossary: "Other Ingredients")
½ cup heavy cream
2 tablespoons sour cream
2 tablespoons olive oil
1 tablespoon lemon juice
2 cloves garlic, minced
¼ cup packed fresh basil
Salt and freshly ground pepper (optional)

FUSILLI SALAD WITH CREAMY BASIL DRESSING

• Cook pasta according to package directions until tender. Drain. Place in mixing bowl with diced red and yellow peppers, onion, pine nuts and mix well. In blender or food processor, combine heavy cream, sour cream, olive oil, lemon juice, garlic and basil and blend thoroughly.
• Pour over pasta mixture and toss until well coated. Add salt and pepper to taste, if desired. Serve chilled or at room temperature.

3 servings.

Serve with: Homemade Chinese Breadsticks (page 154) or sprinkle with toasted canned chow mein noodles.

Variations: Use toasted peanuts or cashews in place of pine nuts; use ½ cup each plain yogurt and low fat milk in place of heavy and sour creams; use fresh parsley in place of fresh basil.

CHINESE CABBAGE PATCH SALAD

1 pound firm tofu
1 10-ounce package bean sprouts
2 cups any cabbage, thinly sliced on angle (1 cup bok choy and 1 cup Chinese cabbage is a good combination)
½ cup thinly sliced mushrooms
¼ cup thinly sliced radishes
1 cup mixed leafy greens

DRESSING:

⅔ cup oil
⅓ cup cider vinegar
¼ cup soy sauce
2 tablespoons grated fresh ginger

• Drain tofu and cut in ¼-inch cubes. Combine dressing ingredients and marinate tofu in dressing 10 minutes.
• Add bean sprouts and sliced cabbage, mushrooms and radishes to tofu and dressing and marinate 10 minutes more, tossing twice. Transfer to serving bowl lined with mixed leafy greens.

4 servings.

Serve with: Chinese Chips (page 148), puffy shrimp chips or chow mein noodles from the can.

Variations: Substitute Red, White and Blue Pepper and Cheese Dressing (page 138) for dressing given; try substituting 1 cup shredded green cabbage and 1 cup shredded iceberg lettuce for the cabbage combination; for nonvegetarian salad, use 2 cups diced shrimp, lobster or crabmeat in place of tofu.

2 large bunches arugula, leaves only
3 to 4 heads Belgian endive
1½ tablespoons minced fresh parsley
1 teaspoon chopped fresh basil or ½ teaspoon dried basil
1 cup cooked or canned beans (such as soybeans, pinto beans, chick-peas), well drained
1 small clove garlic, crushed
½ teaspoon coarse salt
1 teaspoon Dijon-style mustard
Juice of ½ lemon
½ cup vegetable or olive oil
2 teaspoons red wine vinegar
½ teaspoon freshly ground pepper
1 tablespoon slivered lemon peel
Anchovy strips for garnish (optional)

ARUGULA/ ENDIVE SALAD

• Wash arugula well and dry on paper towels. Place the leaves in a salad bowl. Cut endive into quarters lengthwise. Cut lengthwise into strips about ¼-inch wide, place around the greens in bowl. Sprinkle with parsley and basil. Spoon beans into center.
• Mash garlic with salt in a small bowl until the mixture forms a paste. Stir in mustard and lemon juice and whisk in oil, vinegar and pepper.
• Toss salad with dressing just before serving, adding slivered lemon peel as you toss. Garnish if desired with anchovy strips.

4 servings.

Serve with: 20-Calorie Potato Shells (page 160) or salt-free chips and vegetable sticks on the side.

Variations: Substitute broiled and chilled cubes of tofu for beans; substitute oil-free dressing (page 131) of choice for dressing given.

TUNISIAN CARROT SALAD

1 pound carrots, trimmed and scraped
Pinch of salt
2 teaspoons crushed dried mint
Freshly ground pepper, to taste
1 tablespoon olive oil
1 clove garlic, crushed or finely minced
1 tablespoon cider vinegar
12 capers or Homemade Capers (page 169)
Salt or substitute, to taste
Bibb, Boston or any leafy lettuce, cleaned and
separated in leaves
2 hard-boiled eggs, peeled and sliced
1 small ripe tomato, thinly sliced
6 oil-cured black olives

• Slice carrots into ½-inch slices. Place in saucepan, add cold water to cover and pinch of salt. Bring to a boil and simmer 5 minutes, until almost tender. Drain and let cool.
• Transfer carrots to a food processor or blender and blend until coarsely chopped (not a paste). Scrape the mixture into a bowl.
• Add mint, pepper, oil, garlic, vinegar, capers and salt. Blend well and chill.
• Line a salad bowl with lettuce leaves. Spoon carrot salad into center. Garnish with eggs, tomato and olives.

4 servings.

Serve with: Cheesy Eggplant Sticks (page 152).

Variations: Instead of eggs and tomatoes, try tofu squares and red bell pepper strips; substitute shredded red radishes and celery for carrots.

4 medium carrots, peeled and shredded
1 medium unpeeled zucchini, shredded
⅓ cup buttermilk
1 tablespoon coarsely chopped onion
2 teaspoons snipped fresh dill
1 teaspoon Dijon-style mustard
1 teaspoon vinegar
⅛ teaspoon salt or substitute
1 cup cubed cheese of your choice
3 cups mixed greens

PICNIC COLESLAW

• Mix all ingredients except greens by shaking in a container with a tight lid and chill.
• Put washed greens in a plastic bag and chill until picnic time.
• Pack separately and combine vegetables and greens when serving.

3–4 servings.

Serve with: Salad Sprinkles (page 150) of your choice, toasted sunflower seeds or canned chow mein noodles.

Variations: Use shredded jícama or a white turnip in place of the zucchini; try grated parsnips in place of carrots; add ½ cup raisins or currants for variety.

WHOLE MEAL COLESLAW*

½ cup bulgur (cracked) wheat
1 cup water
½ teaspoon salt or substitute, to taste
½ cup mayonnaise
3 tablespoons cider vinegar
¼ teaspoon hot pepper sauce
¼ teaspoon dill
¼ teaspoon Dijon-style mustard
½ cup thinly sliced scallions
1 cup cooked split peas
1½ cups shredded cabbage
½ cup thinly sliced celery
½ cup sliced carrot
  Salad Sprinkles (page 150)

• In a pan, combine the wheat, water, and ½ teaspoon salt; bring to a boil. Stir, cover and simmer 15 minutes, drain and set aside.
• Stir together mayonnaise, vinegar, hot pepper sauce, dill, mustard and scallions.
• Blend dressing into the hot cooked wheat.
• Add peas, cover, and chill well.
• One hour before serving combine the wheat mixture with the next three ingredients.
• Adjust seasoning and spoon mixture into a salad bowl, cover and chill until serving time. Top with Salad Sprinkles.

4 servings.

Serve with: Salad Doodles (page 147).

Variation: Use cooked brown rice in place of bulgur.

*A good picnic salad. Refrigerated, it will keep 7 to 10 days.

SEAFOOD SALADS

½ pound fresh green beans, trimmed
4 carrots (about ¾ pound) trimmed and scraped
3 ribs celery hearts
1 yellow squash
1 zucchini
   Pinch of salt (optional)
1 tablespoon Dijon-style mustard
2 teaspoons white wine vinegar
1 teaspoon lemon juice
½ cup peanut, vegetable or corn oil
   Salt or substitute, to taste
   Freshly ground pepper, to taste
   Red-tip leafy lettuce or romaine, rinsed, dried and
      separated into leaves
4 cups cooked lobster meat in bite-sized pieces
1 cup mayonnaise or Handmade Mayonnaise
   (page 133)

LOBSTER AND VEGETABLE SALAD

• Cut the green beans into ½-inch lengths. Cut carrots lengthwise into strips ¼-inch wide, then cut the strips into ¼-inch dice. Prepare celery, squash, and zucchini the same way.
• Place beans, carrots and celery in a kettle, add cold water to cover, and pinch of salt, if desired. Bring to a boil and simmer 6 minutes.
• Add the squash and zucchini and cook 3 minutes more, drain vegetables well. Place in a bowl and set aside.
• Put the mustard, vinegar and lemon juice in a small bowl and whisk together while gradually adding oil. Add salt or substitute and pepper. Add dressing to vegetables and toss to blend.
• Arrange lettuce leaves on a serving dish. Spoon the vegetables on top, then add lobster. Pass the mayonnaise on the side.

4 servings.

Serve with: Ruffled salt-free snack chips or Pumpkin-seed Salad Wafers (page 153).

Variations: Substitute cubes of cooked monkfish ("poor man's lobster") or swordfish for lobster.

MOLDED LOBSTER SALAD

2 packages (9 or 10 ounces) frozen rock lobster tails
1 cup chopped celery
½ cup chopped cucumber
2 tablespoons lemon juice
2 envelopes unflavored gelatin
2 cups cold water
3 chicken or vegetable bouillon cubes
1½ cups boiling water
2 tablespoons chopped pimiento
1 teaspoon grated onion
4 cups green or red-tip leafy lettuce
1 cup mayonnaise or any other thick dressing
2 hard-boiled eggs, cut in wedges

• Cook lobster tails according to package directions. Remove meat from shells and cut into chunks. Mix with celery and cucumber. Sprinkle with lemon juice. Cover and chill.

• Sprinkle gelatin on ½ cup of the cold water, let soften 5 minutes. Combine gelatin, bouillon cubes and boiling water in mixing bowl. Stir until gelatin and cubes are completely dissolved. Mix in remaining 1½ cups cold water. Chill until mixture reaches the consistency of unbeaten egg white.

• Combine lobster mixture, pimiento and onion. Fold into thickened gelatin. Pour into 1½ quart ring mold. Chill until set. Unmold on serving platter lined with greens. Fill center with mayonnaise and garnish with hard-boiled eggs.

4 servings.

Serve with: Plain bread and Fancy Butter (page 155) or toasted oyster crackers.

Variations: Substitute crabmeat for lobster; substitute diced red bell pepper for pimientos.

2 medium-size heads of any loose leaf lettuce
1 cup cooked lobster meat
3 tablespoons clarified butter
1 teaspoon lemon juice
1 clove garlic, minced
3 tablespoons olive oil
⅔ cup cooked white rice
1 sprig rosemary, snipped, or 1 teaspoon dried
    rosemary
  Freshly ground pepper, to taste
1½ cups grated Swiss cheese

LOBSTER AND LETTUCE SALAD WITH MELTED BUTTER DRESSING

• Clean and dry lettuce well. Separate leaves and add whole to salad bowl.
• Cut lobster into bite-sized pieces.
• Combine over low heat the clarified butter, lemon juice, garlic and oil.
• Stir in lobster and rice. Add rosemary and mix well. Remove from heat, let cool to lukewarm, then spoon over greens. Toss well. Grind pepper on top, sprinkle with grated cheese and serve at once.

3 servings.

Serve with: Melba toast or Pumpkinseed Salad Wafers (page 153).

Variations: Use finely shredded cabbage (about 5 to 6 cups) instead of lettuce; monkfish or swordfish in place of lobster; use wild rice or brown rice in place of white rice.

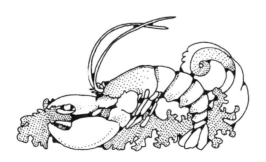

CRABMEAT SALAD WITH LIME VINAIGRETTE
(a composed salad)

2 small heads radicchio
2 heads Bibb lettuce
1 bunch watercress
1½ to 2 cups cooked crabmeat
4 Belgian endives, trimmed
1 cup chopped fresh basil leaves (optional)
   Lime Vinaigrette (page 130)

• Separate radicchio and Bibb leaves; rinse, drain well. Set aside about 10 of the radicchio leaves; tear remaining leaves into 1-inch pieces.
• Cut endives lengthwise into quarters; cut each quarter lengthwise into ¼-inch strips. Remove stems from watercress; rinse leaves, then drain well.
• Arrange reserved whole radicchio leaves around edge of a large serving platter. Combine torn lettuce and watercress and place in center of platter. Lump crabmeat on top and make a border of the endive strips around lettuce and watercress; sprinkle with basil leaves.
• Just before serving, whisk vinaigrette and pour over salad. Toss at the table.

4 servings.

Serve with: Herb Wheels (page 152) or sesame breadsticks.

Variations: Use escarole in place of the radicchio; use romaine in place of endive; substitute fresh mint or flat leaf parsley for basil.

1 bunch watercress, coarsely chopped
1½ cups cooked crabmeat
1 clove garlic, finely chopped
2 to 3 teaspoons powdered ginger
2 tablespoons soy sauce
2 tablespoons sesame oil
2 tablespoons cider vinegar
½ teaspoon fresh ground pepper
1 cup shredded head lettuce
  Salad Sprinkles (page 150) of your choice

HOT CRESS AND CRAB SALAD

• Steam coarsely chopped watercress until slightly wilted. Mix with crabmeat and set aside.
• Combine the next six ingredients.
• Arrange lettuce on individual serving plates, top with cooked cress and crab.
• Add salad dressing and Salad Sprinkles.

2 servings.

Serve with: Super Salad Croissants (page 159) or melba toast.

Variations: Substitute sorrel or arugula for watercress; replace ground pepper with 1 teaspoon bottled green peppercorns.

TUNA AND BROCCOLI SALAD

1 small head broccoli
2 6½-ounce cans solid white tuna, drained and cut
    into bite-sized chunks
  Juice of 1 lemon or lime
½ cup chopped red onion
½ cup chopped celery
¾ cup mayonnaise
2 tablespoons water
  Salt or substitute, to taste
  Freshly ground pepper, to taste
3 cups Boston or any other soft-leafed lettuce,
    washed, dried and chilled

• Cut broccoli into small flowerets, saving stems for another use. Place flowerets in a steamer or pot of boiling water. Cook 3 minutes or until crisp-tender. Drain, rinse in cold water, set aside.
• Mix tuna with lemon juice, onion and celery. Stir in broccoli.
• Thin mayonnaise with the water and season with salt and pepper. Fold the mayonnaise into the fish mixture.
• Serve over a bed of the lettuce.

4 servings.

Serve with: Shrimp chips, oyster crackers or Roaster's Choice Croutons (page 147).

Variations: Use cubes of cooked firm-textured fish such as monkfish, halibut or swordfish in place of the tuna; use cauliflower in place of broccoli.

1 15½-ounce can white kidney beans
2 small tomatoes, quartered
1 small red onion, thinly sliced
¼ cup minced parsley
2 tablespoons minced, pitted black olives
¼ teaspoon fresh-cracked pepper
1 small head radicchio or red leaf lettuce
¼ pound arugula or young dandelion leaves
1 7-ounce can water-packed tuna, drained
3 tablespoons olive oil
2 tablespoons red wine vinegar
2 cloves garlic, minced
½ teaspoon Dijon-style mustard
¼ teaspoon oregano

SALAD NIÇOISE WITH WHITE BEANS AND TUNA

• Rinse kidney beans in a colander; drain.
• Place beans in a bowl with tomatoes, onion, parsley, olives and pepper.
• Mix last five ingredients in a separate bowl.
• Add half of the dressing to the bean mixture; toss gently to mix.
• Arrange radicchio and arugula in the center of a large serving platter.
• Spoon the beans around the center, then arrange the tuna around the beans.
• Drizzle remaining dressing over tuna and serve.

4 servings.

Serve with: 20-Calorie Potato Shells (page 160) or unsalted nuts and raw peas.

Variation: Use drained canned mackerel in place of tuna; if you garden, comfrey leaves are a good substitute for store-bought dandelion greens.

TUNA-MELON SALAD

½ medium size head lettuce (any kind), washed, dried
   and shredded
1½ cups diced cantaloupe or honeydew melon
 1 cup orange or tangerine sections
 1 6½-ounce can white tuna, drained and flaked
½ cup sliced scallions
 1 3-ounce can pitted ripe olives, sliced
¼ cup chopped celery
½ cup mayonnaise
 1 tablespoon lemon or lime juice

• In salad bowl combine lettuce, melon, orange, tuna, scallions, olives and celery. Chill.
• Immediately before serving, combine mayonnaise and lemon juice, mix with salad and ingredients and toss well.

4–6 servings.

Serve with: Thin slices of homemade Pesto Presto Salad Bread (page 154) or sliced party pumpernickel with a 30-Second Salad Spread (page 156) of your choice.

Variations: Substitute crabmeat for tuna; use chopped water chestnuts in place of celery.

1 small head broccoli
1 tablespoon red wine vinegar
¼ cup Dijon-style mustard
  Freshly ground pepper
  Salt or substitute, to taste
1 tablespoon chopped fresh dill
1 cup oil (a blend of olive and vegetable is best)
1½ cups steamed or smoked scallops
1½ cups shredded iceberg lettuce

BROCCOLI-SCALLOP SALAD

• Cut off and discard the bottom 2 inches of broccoli stem. Separate remainder into flowerets with stems attached. Bring a pot of salted (if desired) water to a boil, add broccoli and cook 4 minutes. Drain in a colander and spread the pieces out on a kitchen towel to cool and dry.
• In a food processor or blender combine the vinegar, mustard, pepper, salt or substitute and dill. With the motor running, gradually add oil. (The sauce will be thick as mayonnaise.)
• Arrange broccoli and scallops in a shallow serving bowl lined with shredded lettuce. Spoon on dressing. Let stand at least an hour at room temperature to improve flavor before serving.

3 servings.

Serve with: Individual snack cups of toasted pistachios or pine nuts.

Variations: Substitute cauliflower for broccoli; substitute fresh coriander or tarragon for dill; top with Goldenrod Garnish (page 146).

SHRIMP AND ORANGE SALAD WITH ROSEMARY VINAIGRETTE

1 cup chopped celery
  Salt or substitute
3 oranges, peeled and sliced
1½ pounds shrimp
1 bunch watercress, rinsed and drained
2 tablespoons red wine vinegar
6 tablespoons olive oil
½ teaspoon paprika
  Salt or substitute, to taste
  Freshly ground pepper, to taste
½ teaspoon minced garlic
1 teaspoon chopped fresh rosemary leaves,
    or ½ teaspoon dried

• Put the celery in a saucepan with cold water to cover and salt to taste. Bring to a boil, and simmer 30 minutes. Drain, set aside to cool.
• Arrange alternating overlapping slices of oranges with shrimp on bed of watercress. Top with chopped celery.
• Blend vinegar with oil, paprika, salt, pepper, garlic and rosemary. Spoon over the salad and serve at room temperature.

4 servings.

Serve with: Shrimp Chips or Homemade Chinese Breadsticks (page 154).

Variations: Substitute parsley for watercress; use 1 cup lightly steamed, chilled and chopped broccoli or 1 cup cubed raw jícama instead of celery.

DELUXE SHRIMP SALAD

  2 cups shredded raw parsnips
  1 cup finely sliced celery or celery root
  1 tablespoon chopped pimiento or red bell pepper
  ½ cup minced green olive or ¼ cup bottled green
      peppercorns, drained
  ½ cup Handmade Mayonnaise (page 133)
  1 tablespoon fresh lemon juice
  2 teaspoons finely sliced scallion
  ¾ teaspoon salt or substitute
      Freshly ground black or white pepper, to taste
  1 cup kale, mustard greens, or other dark leafy green
  2 cups shredded, red or green cabbage
  1½ cups cooked cocktail-size shrimp

• Mix first 4 ingredients and set aside.
• Blend mayonnaise, lemon juice, scallion, salt and pepper.
• Combine with first mixture and mound on a bed of the
greens mixed with the cabbage. Top with shrimp.

3 servings.

Serve with: 20-Calorie Potato Shells (page 160) or ruffled
potato chips.

Variations: Use a yogurt or tofu dressing for mayonnaise
(see list on page 137); use ½ cup peppery-flavored radish
sprouts in place of ground pepper.

SNOW PEA SEAFOOD SALAD

2 red bell peppers (about ¾ pound)
1 cup cooked small salad shrimp or crabmeat
  Pinch of salt or substitute
¾ pound snow peas, trimmed
1 small red onion, thinly sliced
1 tablespoon prepared mustard
2 tablespoons red wine vinegar
  Salt or substitute, to taste
  Freshly ground pepper, to taste
¼ cup olive oil
¼ cup minced parsley
1 cup any soft leaf lettuce torn into bite-sized pieces

• Preheat broiler to high or heat charcoal grill. Place peppers under broiler or on grill and cook on all sides until skin is well charred. When cool enough to handle split in half, core and discard charred skin.

• Cut peppers lengthwise into thin strips. There should be about 1 cup. Put strips in salad bowl. Add shrimp.

• Bring enough water to a boil to cover peas when added. Add pinch of salt. Add peas and boil 2 minutes. Drain, rinse and cool. Add to shrimp mixture.

• Add onion to shrimp.

• Combine mustard, vinegar, salt and pepper in a small bowl. Whisk vigorously, adding oil gradually. Stir in parsley.

• Add dressing to shrimp salad, toss and serve over lettuce arranged on individual plates.

2–3 servings.

Serve with: Super Salad Croissants (page 159) or plain bread and Fancy Butter (page 155) on the side.

Variations: Substitute green peppers for red; use white wine vinegar in place of red and sesame oil in place of olive oil; use 1 cup cooked diced lobster or monkfish instead of shrimp.

ARUGULA SEAFOOD SALAD

3 cups arugula
1 head Boston lettuce
1 small red onion, thinly sliced or grated
1½ cups cooked shrimp or crabmeat
1 teaspoon grated orange rind
2 tablespoons orange juice
2 tablespoons lemon juice
¾ teaspoon salt or substitute
¼ teaspoon coarsely ground black pepper
2 tablespoons snipped parsley, chives or scallion greens
⅓ cup olive oil
¼ teaspoon curry powder

• Tear arugula and lettuce into bite-sized pieces. In a large salad bowl, combine with onion and seafood, cover and chill.
• To make dressing, combine all remaining ingredients in a small bowl or glass jar. Spoon over salad and toss until greens are well coated.

4 servings.

Serve with: Bacon bits or Fake Bacon Bits (page 147) and raw red and green bell pepper slices.

Variations: Use Bibb lettuce in place of Boston; use watercress instead of arugula; substitute Thick and Creamy Mustard Dressing (page 136) for dressing given.

MUSSEL, SHRIMP AND SCALLOP SALAD WITH MANGO

6 cups (about 2 pounds) fresh mussels
2 cups water or vegetable broth
½ teaspoon dried thyme
1 bay leaf
2 tablespoons white wine vinegar
1 pint fresh sea scallops (about 3 cups)
8 large shrimp (about ¼ pound), peeled and deveined
   Salt or substitute, to taste
½ pound snow peas, trimmed
1 unblemished ripe mango (about 1 pound)
1 small head Chinese cabbage or romaine lettuce, shredded (about 6 cups)
½ cup finely chopped scallions
¾ cup any vinaigrette dressing
½ cup finely chopped mixed herbs, such as parsley, chives and basil

• Scrub the mussels well and put in a kettle with water or vegetable broth. Add thyme, bay leaf and vinegar. Cover tightly, bring to a boil and cook 3 minutes, until mussels open. Discard any mussels that do not open.

• Strain cooking liquid from mussels through a cheesecloth-lined sieve (there should be about ½ cup).

• Put liquid in a clean saucepan, add scallops, cover and bring to a boil. Simmer 1 minute. Add shrimp and salt. Cook another minute. Remove from heat. Drain.

• Remove the mussels from the shells.

• Place snow peas in a saucepan, add cold water to cover. Bring to a boil and simmer 2 minutes. Drain.

• Peel mango. Cut the flesh away from the stone and slice into ½-inch cubes.

• In a large bowl, combine cabbage, mango, snow peas and scallions. Add ¼ cup of the vinaigrette and toss to blend.

• Put tossed mixture on a large platter. Arrange mussels, scallops and shrimp on top. Spoon the remaining vinaigrette over the seafood. Sprinkle with chopped herbs.

4 servings.

Serve with: Crusty garlic bread or Vegetable Crisps (page 155).

Variations: Use canned, drained mussels (about 2 cups) in place of fresh; use 1½ pounds shrimp and no scallops; substitute 1 pound ripe, firm peaches (peeled) for the mango.

SEAFOOD SALAD WITH ANCHOVY DRESSING

1 head cauliflower (about 1 pound)
2 zucchini (about ½ pound)
3 carrots (about ½ pound), trimmed and scraped
1 cup canned and drained mussels or minced clams
4 teaspoons Dijon-style mustard
1 teaspoon anchovy paste
3 tablespoons red wine vinegar
  Freshly ground pepper, to taste
6 tablespoons olive oil
1 cup torn spinach leaves or romaine lettuce

• Cut flowerets from the heavier stems of the cauliflower stalks. Cut stems in half (trim or scrape the heavier stems) and cut into bite-size pieces.
• Cut zucchini crosswise into 1½-inch slices and cut each into quarters.
• Slice carrots into ¼-inch rounds. Place in saucepan, add cold water to cover, bring to a boil; simmer 3 minutes. Drain.
• Meanwhile, cover cauliflower and zucchini with water. Cook until crisp-tender; drain. Combine with drained mussels or clams.
• Put mustard in a mixing bowl, add the anchovy paste, vinegar and pepper. Stir vigorously with a wire whisk while adding the oil.
• Transfer vegetables and mussels to a salad bowl. Add anchovy dressing and torn spinach. Toss gently and serve.

2–3 servings.

Serve with: 1-2-3 Melba Toast (page 151) or assorted salt-free crackers and dry-roasted nuts.

Variations: Omit anchovies. Substitute soybean miso or sundried tomato paste (both available from health food and gourmet food shops); substitute yellow summer squash for zucchini.

SALMON-STUFFED ENDIVE

3 to 4 Belgian endives
1 can (6½ or 7 ounces) salmon, drained and flaked
¼ cup mayonnaise
¼ cup plain yogurt
¼ teaspoon lemon juice
¼ teaspoon curry powder, or to taste

• Carefully detach each endive leaf from the head, rinse and pat dry. Combine the salmon, mayonnaise, yogurt, lemon juice and curry powder.
• Spread a spoonful or two of salmon on each leaf. Chill before serving.

3–4 servings.

Serve with: Vegetable Crisps (page 155) or taco chips on the side.

Variations: Substitute chicken breast or white tuna for salmon.

FIDDLER'S GREENS

2 crisp heads of Boston or butter lettuce
½ cup fresh minced parsley
1 cup fresh, steamed fiddlehead ferns*
½ cup thinly sliced smoked salmon, cut into strips

• Toss together the lettuce, parsley and ferns.
• Top with salmon and toss with Lemon or Lime Vinaigrette (pages 41, 130).

3–4 servings.

Serve with: Super Salad Croissants (page 159) or rye breadsticks.

Variation: Garnish with slices of kiwi before serving.

---

*These tightly curled shoots of young ferns poke up through the forest floor in early spring and unfurl into full, feathery form almost overnight. The fiddlehead fern season lasts only a few brief weeks. Fiddleheads are so called because the unopened fern looks like the end of a violin. They come from as far south as Georgia and, as the weather warms, the season shifts northward. They are also available canned.

MOZZARELLA PLUS SALAD

    2 tablespoons minced basil
    1 tablespoon minced parsley
    1 large clove garlic, peeled and minced
    5 tablespoons olive oil
 1½ teaspoons red wine vinegar
      Salt and freshly ground black pepper, to taste
 3½ cups mixed greens (such as Boston, spinach,
        escarole)
    4 large ripe tomatoes, sliced ¼-inch thick
    8 ounces mozzarella cheese, sliced
  ½ cup toasted cashews or walnut halves
    1 red onion, peeled and sliced into fine rings
    1 can flat anchovy fillets, well drained
      Garnish: fresh parsley sprigs, oil-cured black olives

• In a blender combine the basil, parsley, garlic, oil, vinegar; season with a pinch of salt and pepper.
• Blend until smooth; set dressing aside.
• On a large rectangular platter arrange the greens, then alternate the tomato and mozzarella slices in rows on top, overlapping the slices decoratively.
• Spoon the dressing over the salad.
• Add a grinding of black pepper, top with red onion rings, nuts and decorative design of anchovy fillets.
• Garnish with parsley sprigs and oil-cured olives. Serve slightly chilled.

4 servings.

Serve with: Dry roasted nuts or Nutty Mix (page 148).

Variations: Substitute 8 ounces lean, thinly sliced corned beef or prosciutto; use 1 cup finely shredded cabbage in place of 1 cup lettuce.

CACTUS CRABMEAT SALAD

8 ounces fresh cactus leaves (see page 32)
1 cup cooked, chilled crabmeat
2 medium-sized ripe or green tomatoes, cored and diced
1 tablespoon sesame or safflower oil
1 teaspoon white wine vinegar
¼ teaspoon salt or substitute
⅛ teaspoon freshly ground pepper
1 tablespoon finely chopped parsley or mint
2 cups any leaf lettuce

• Using a small sharp knife or vegetable peeler, carefully remove the thorns from the cactus leaves. Trim about ¼ inch from each leaf all the way around.
• On a cutting board, cut cactus leaves into ½-inch dice. Place in a saucepan, cover with boiling water and cook until tender, about 10 minutes. Drain well.
• Combine drained cactus with crabmeat, diced tomatoes, oil, vinegar, salt, pepper and parsley. Mix, chill and serve spooned over greens.

2 servings.

Serve with: 30-Second Salad Spread (page 156) of your choice on assorted crackers.

Variations: Substitute diced green or red pepper for cactus; substitute small shrimp for crabmeat; for a vegetarian version, substitute 1 cup Homemade Vegetable Protein (pages 35, 36) or 1 cup coarsely grated mozzarella cheese for the crabmeat.

POULTRY SALADS

2 cups cooked chicken in bite-sized cubes
4 scallions, chopped
½ cup finely chopped walnuts
¼ cup fresh basil leaves, torn into small pieces
½ cup walnut oil
¼ cup safflower (or peanut) oil
¼ cup raspberry or red wine vinegar, or to taste
Salt or substitute, to taste
Freshly ground pepper, to taste
3½ cups mixed salad greens (such as watercress,
endive, red leaf lettuce, radicchio, Boston lettuce,
arugula)
2 tablespoons chopped fresh chives

CHICKEN SALAD WITH WALNUT VINAIGRETTE

• Place chicken in a mixing bowl and add scallions, walnuts and basil.
• In a small bowl, combine the oils and vinegar. Blend well and season with salt and pepper.
• Put the salad greens in a large bowl and toss with enough dressing to coat the leaves. Distribute among four individual plates.
• Place the chicken on the greens. Stir chives into the remaining dressing and spoon over chicken.

4 servings.

Serve with: Plain bread and Fancy Butter (page 155) or chilled carrot curls and cheese cubes.

Variations: Use cooked turkey, duck or Cornish hen in place of chicken; substitute leeks or shallots for scallions; substitute fresh parsley or dill for chives.

HOT SNAP BEAN SALAD

2 tablespoons Dijon-style mustard
1 tablespoon red wine vinegar
1 tablespoon lemon juice
6 tablespoons olive oil
½ pound green or yellow wax beans, trimmed and French-cut
1 small red pepper, seeded and cut into thin strips
Salt or substitute, to taste
1 tablespoon sweet butter
1 scallion, minced
1 clove garlic, minced
¼ pound thinly sliced prosciutto, cut into strips
1 tablespoon chopped fresh basil or mint
2 cups cubed cooked chicken or turkey
1½ cups shredded iceberg lettuce

• Whisk the mustard with the vinegar and lemon juice in a small bowl until smooth. Slowly whisk in the oil. Cover and refrigerate 1 hour.

• Cook the beans and pepper in boiling salted water for about 3 minutes. Drain.

• Melt the butter in a large skillet over medium heat. Add the scallion and cook 1 minute. Add garlic; cook 3 minutes more.

• Add the drained beans, prosciutto, basil and chicken. Cook, stirring, until warmed through.

• Transfer to salad bowl lined with the shredded lettuce. Spoon on dressing, toss and serve warm.

3 servings.

Serve with: Super Salad Croissants (page 159), Fruit-Filled Croissants (page 160) or unsalted mixed nuts.

Variations: Substitute Lime Vinaigrette (page 130) or a homemade mayonnaise (pages 133–135) for dressing given.

CABBAGE PATCH SLAW

¼ cup mayonnaise
¼ cup milk
2 teaspoons lemon or lime juice
½ teaspoon salt or substitute
⅛ teaspoon freshly ground pepper
4 cups shredded green or red cabbage
1 cup quartered pitted dates or prunes (or ⅔ cup raisins), plumped*
1 cup slivered roasted turkey or chicken
¼ cup toasted slivered almonds
1 cup torn romaine, iceberg or other crisp lettuce

• In a large bowl, blend together mayonnaise, milk, lemon juice, salt and pepper.
• Add cabbage and dates, toss to coat all; chill 30 minutes.
• Add turkey, sprinkle with almonds. Serve over lettuce.

2–3 servings.

Serve with: Super Salad Croissants (page 159) or buttered toasted English muffins.

Variations: Use roast pork in place of poultry. To reduce calories, use ⅔ cup chopped dried apples or pears, plumped, in place of dates or prunes.

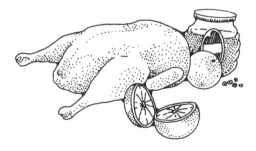

*To "plump" place fruit in a saucepan and add enough hot water (or herb tea) to cover. Bring to a boil. Remove from heat; steep for 10-15 minutes. Drain and pat dry. When cool, fruit is ready to be used.

SLIVERED CHICKEN LIVER SALAD

¼ cup olive or salad oil
3 tablespoons lemon juice
½ teaspoon salt or substitute
½ teaspoon sugar (optional)
¼ teaspoon dried chervil
¼ teaspoon dried thyme
¼ teaspoon dry mustard
⅛ teaspoon white or black pepper
5 cups loosely packed chicory
1 small red or white onion, thinly sliced or grated
1 cup small macaroni shells, cooked and cooled
1 cup thinly sliced celery
¼ cup minced parsley
1 tablespoon olive or salad oil
1 tablespoon butter
1 pound whole chicken livers

• Combine ¼ cup olive oil, lemon juice, salt, sugar, chervil, thyme, mustard and pepper; cover and set aside.
• In a large salad bowl, combine the chicory, onion, macaroni, celery and parsley. Cover and chill 2 to 4 hours.
• Just before serving, heat 1 tablespoon olive oil and butter in a large frying pan over medium-high heat. Add livers and cook until browned on all sides but still pink in the center. Cool briefly and cut into thin slivers. Return to pan, stir to coat and add to salad mixture. Stir dressing and pour over salad. Toss to mix well and serve at once.

4 servings.

Serve with: Pumpkinseed Salad Wafers (page 153), garlic croutons (page 145) or seeded breadsticks.

Variations: Substitute calf liver or diced kidney for chicken liver; use sliced water chestnuts in place of celery; use leeks in place of onion. For vegetarian version, substitute 2 cups tofu or Homemade Vegetable Protein (pages 35, 36) for the liver.

2 cups (4 ounces) macaroni shells
2 large fresh broccoli stalks
2 tablespoons chopped fresh basil (or 2 teaspoons dried)
2 teaspoons chopped fresh oregano (or ⅔ teaspoon dried)
5 tablespoons olive oil
4 tablespoons red wine vinegar
4 tablespoons grated onion
2 medium tomatoes, cubed
1 cup cubed poultry (chicken, turkey, game hen or duck)
  Salt or substitute and freshly ground black pepper
1 cup shredded head lettuce
1 cup torn arugula, radicchio or dandelion greens

PASTA PRESTO SALAD

• Bring 2–3 quarts salted water to boil in covered pot. Cook shells 7 minutes. Drain; rinse until cool.

• Bring hot water to boil in steamer. Remove tough stems from broccoli and cut heads into flowerets. Steam broccoli about 5 minutes, depending on size of flowerets. Drain broccoli and rinse under cold water until cool.

• Chop fresh basil and oregano.

• Beat together the oil and vinegar and add the basil, oregano and grated onion.

• Combine broccoli, tomatoes, macaroni and poultry. Mix in dressing, season to taste and serve warm over a mixture of the shredded lettuce and torn greens.

2–3 servings.

Serve with: Herb Wheels (page 152) or garlic-buttered clover-leaf rolls.

Variations: Substitute fresh fettucine for dried macaroni shells; for seafood version, substitute one 7-ounce can water-packed albacore tuna, drained and rinsed, for the poultry.

RED, WHITE AND GREEN SUMMER SALAD

3 tablespoons Dijon-style mustard
⅓ cup sherry wine vinegar
½ cup olive oil
2 whole boned chicken breasts (about 1½ pounds)
2 sweet red peppers
1 large green pepper
1 teaspoon minced fresh green chili peppers
2 tablespoons minced scallions
2 tablespoons minced flat-leaf parsley
  Salt or substitute and freshly ground black pepper, to taste
3 cups mixed greens

• Mix mustard with two tablespoons of the vinegar and one tablespoon of the oil. Brush this mixture on the chicken and allow to marinate at room temperature for 15 minutes.
• Core and seed the peppers and quarter them lengthwise. Brush with a little of the oil.
• Preheat grill or oven broiler and broil the chicken and peppers for 20 minutes, turning once, until browned and cooked through. The chicken and peppers should be grilled at some distance from the source of heat so they don't char.
• Carve chicken against the grain in ½-inch-thick slices. Slice the peppers into strips ½-inch wide.
• Combine remaining vinegar and oil.
• In a shallow serving bowl, mix chicken, peppers, chili peppers, scallions and parsley.
• Toss with oil and vinegar; season to taste. Spoon over greens just before serving.

3 servings.

Serve with: Cream cheese balls rolled in toasted walnuts or poppyseed; or with sesame breadsticks.

Variations: Substitute grilled turkey or game hen for chicken breast; use balsamic vinegar in place of sherry wine vinegar.

2 whole chicken breasts, halved and skinned
1 cup cold water
1 small bay leaf
2 cloves garlic
1 tablespoon salad oil
4 scallions, minced
1 tablespoon soy sauce
1 tablespoon minced fresh ginger or 1 teaspoon
    cayenne
1 teaspoon cornstarch
¼ cup cold water
12 leaves romaine lettuce

CHICKEN WRAPPED IN ROMAINE LEAVES

• Place chicken breasts in a skillet in 1 cup cold water with the bay leaf and whole garlic. Simmer, covered, for 20 minutes or until done.

• Remove chicken from skillet, reserving cooking liquid. When cool enough to handle, remove the chicken meat from the bones and shred or chop into small pieces.

• Heat the oil in a large skillet and sauté the scallions until limp. Add soy sauce, ginger, chicken and the reserved cooking liquid. Cook 3-4 minutes over high heat, stirring often. Dissolve the cornstarch in the cold water, stir into chicken mixture and simmer until thickened slightly.

• Place one spoonful of chicken on each romaine leaf and roll it up to be eaten out of hand like an egg roll.

4 servings.

Serve with: Vegetable Crisps (page 155) or taco chips.

Variations: Spoon chicken down the center of the leaves and arrange on serving platter in a sun-burst pattern; garnish with fresh watercress or basil or parsley and top with a tablespoon of dressing of your choice; use salmon or turkey breast in place of chicken.

CHINESE CHICKEN NOODLE SALAD

2 boned chicken breasts, halved
2 cups water, white wine or dry vermouth
3 tablespoons water
2 tablespoons soy sauce
2 tablespoons sesame paste
1½ tablespoons dry sherry
2 teaspoons red wine vinegar
3 medium cloves garlic
   1-inch piece ginger
12 ounces very thin spaghetti or fresh, frozen, or dried
   Chinese noodles
2 teaspoons sesame oil
2 scallions
   Freshly ground black pepper, to taste
3 cups chickory or escarole

• Place chicken in skillet. Pour 2 cups water, wine or vermouth into skillet to cover chicken halfway. Cover and simmer 20 minutes.
• Combine 3 tablespoons water, soy sauce, sesame paste, sherry and vinegar.
• Put garlic through press.
• Mince ginger.
• Add garlic and ginger to soy mixture.
• Bring 3 quarts salted water to boil in covered pot.
• Cook dried noodles about 7 minutes (fresh or about 30 seconds) until tender.
• Drain and rinse. Sprinkle noodles with sesame oil.
• Chop scallions finely.
• Remove chicken from skillet and remove skin. Shred or dice chicken and mix with a small amount of the soy mixture. Set aside.
• Mix noodles with remaining soy mixture. Top with chicken and sprinkle on scallions. Spoon over greens and serve at room temperature.

4 servings.

Serve with: Salad Doodles (page 147) or more toasted dried noodles on the side.

Variations: Substitute natural peanut butter for sesame paste; use 1 cup leftover dark meat of chicken, turkey or game instead of chicken breasts.

1 head romaine lettuce
½ pound dandelion greens
1 bunch arugula
2 tablespoons chopped fresh chives or scallion tops
1 tablespoon chopped fresh parsley
1½ cups cubed cooked chicken
¼ pound Fontina cheese, cut in paper-thin slices and
then julienned
¼ teaspoon salt or substitute
2 teaspoons Dijon-style mustard
1 tablespoon sherry
2 teaspoons tarragon vinegar
1 egg yolk
⅓ cup olive oil
Freshly ground pepper, to taste

SPRING GREENS CHICKEN SALAD

• Remove stems from dandelion greens and arugula. Carefully separate romaine leaves. Wash the leaves well and pat dry. Line a large bowl with the greens and add the chives, parsley, chicken and cheese.

• Whisk the salt with the mustard in a medium bowl. Add the sherry, vinegar, egg yolk, olive oil and pepper. Spoon over salad; toss until well mixed.

4 servings.

Serve with: Fresh dandelion buds on top, crackers or Herb Wheels (page 152) on the side.

Variations: Substitute a homemade flavored vinegar (pages 173–174) for tarragon vinegar; use mustard or turnip greens in place of arugula; for a seafood version, substitute chunks of cooked, cubed tuna, swordfish or monkfish for chicken.

TABOULI 2001

1 cup bulgur (cracked wheat) or 1 cup cooked wild
   rice
1 small cucumber, diced
2 medium tomatoes, diced
1 or 2 scallions with tops, minced
10 radishes, diced or shredded
½ cup thinly sliced smoked turkey or smoked salmon
1 cup torn amaranth, radicchio or arugula
½ cup lemon juice
¼ cup olive oil
1 to 3 teaspoons dried mint
   Salt or salt substitute and freshly ground pepper, to
   taste

• Place bulgur in a bowl, cover with hot water and set aside until cool enough to handle.

• Transfer the bulgur to another bowl a handful at a time, squeezing out as much water as possible between your palms. Let stand three hours.

• Add cucumber, tomatoes, scallions, radishes and sliced turkey to the bulgur. Mix well, then add the greens.

• Combine the lemon juice, olive oil and mint; season with salt and pepper, to taste and add to salad. Toss well.

2–3 servings.

Serve with: Corn chips or Corn Chip Topping (page 145).

Variations: Use fresh chopped spinach, sorrel or watercress as the green; use ½ cup mint vinegar and omit dried mint and lemon juice.

2 small or 1 large head Boston lettuce
1 bunch parsley or watercress, stems removed
1 cup slivered cooked white meat of turkey or
     chicken
3 hard-boiled egg yolks
¾ cup heavy cream
¾ teaspoon salt or substitute
¼ teaspoon coarsely ground black pepper
2 tablespoons lemon juice
½ teaspoon poppy seeds (optional)

BOSTON CREAM SALAD

• Tear well-washed and dried lettuce leaves into large pieces. Place in salad bowl and add watercress. Top with turkey. Chill.
• Mash egg yolks in a small bowl and gradually stir in cream. Add salt and pepper, then stir in lemon juice (drop by drop to prevent cream from curdling).
• Drizzle dressing over salad. Toss gently and serve immediately with poppy seeds sprinkled on top.

3 servings.

Serve with: Super Salad Croissants (page 159) or chilled radish roses and carrot curls (see "Tips for Tossers," page 189).

Variations: Use Bibb lettuce or spinach in place of Boston lettuce; substitute caraway or celery seeds for poppy seeds; use half-and-half or *crème fraîche* in place of heavy cream; for a seafood version, substitute 1 cup cooked crabmeat for the poultry.

CORNISH GAME HEN AND WILD RICE SALAD

1 Cornish game hen, cut in half
  Broth or water
½ pound snow peas, ends trimmed
1 cup cooked wild rice
1 cup thinly sliced celery or water chestnuts
1 small red pepper, cut into thin strips
¼ cup thinly sliced scallions
1 small bunch watercress or parsley, stems trimmed
1 cup shredded cabbage

DRESSING:

2 tablespoons olive oil
¼ cup plain low fat yogurt
4 teaspoons white wine
1 clove garlic, crushed
⅛ teaspoon salt
¼ teaspoon rosemary

• Place hen halves in a skillet with enough water, broth or a mix of both to cover. Bring to a boil, reduce heat and poach 15-20 minutes until cooked through. Cool in liquid and, when cool enough to handle, pull hen meat from the bones, then cut into strips or dice. Place snow peas in ½-inch boiling water, cover and cook 1 minute. Drain and refresh under cold running water.
• Mix chicken, snow peas, rice, celery, pepper and scallions in a bowl.
• Mix dressing, add to salad and toss.
• Arrange watercress or parsley and cabbage on two serving plates. Top with equal amounts of salad; serve immediately.

2 servings.

Serve with: Coriander Crackers (page 153) or Herb Wheels (page 152).

Variations: Use Pecan Dressing (page 53) in place of dressing above; substitute French-cut string beans for snow peas; use brown rice in place of wild rice.

MEAT SALADS

WARM STEAK SALAD WITH SALSA DRESSING

¾ pound lean sirloin steak, trimmed of fat
1 tablespoon olive oil
2 pounds kale or spinach, stems trimmed
1 cup cooked corn
½ small red onion, thinly sliced
1 medium-sized head romaine or Boston lettuce

SALSA DRESSING:

2 large ripe tomatoes, finely chopped
3 jalapeño peppers, seeded and finely chopped
½ small red onion, finely chopped
½ teaspoon salt or substitute
1 teaspoon red wine vinegar
2 tablespoons finely chopped coriander or parsley

• Combine all dressing ingredients. Mix well and set aside.
• Grill or broil steak to desired degree of doneness, then slice thinly.
• Heat oil in a large skillet, add kale and stir-fry 3–4 minutes.
• Transfer kale to a large serving bowl. Add steak, corn and onion slices and toss. Serve over lettuce arranged in individual salad bowls. Spoon on dressing.

3–4 servings.

Serve with: 20-Calorie Potato Shells (page 160) or warm canned potato sticks and cold celery sticks.

Variations: Use arugula or broccoli rabe in place of kale; substitute ¾ pound sautéed tofu strips or slivers of broiled tempeh for the steak.

AU JUS BEEF SALAD WITH MUSTARD VINAIGRETTE

½ pound thinly sliced very rare roast beef
   (approximately 12 slices)
½ cup chopped celery
1 red bell pepper, coarsely chopped
1 medium head romaine leaves, torn
2 tablespoons chopped parsley
½ cup olive oil
1 teaspoon Dijon-style mustard
¼ cup red wine vinegar
2 tablespoons lemon juice
1 tablespoon capers, drained
   Freshly ground pepper

• Cut roast beef into long, thin on-the-bias strips. Place in salad bowl with celery, red pepper, romaine and parsley.
• Combine remaining ingredients and mix well.
• Pour over salad ingredients. Toss and serve.

3 servings.

Serve with: Low-sodium rice cakes or Herb Wheels (page 152).

Variations: Use spinach or chard instead of romaine; substitute Low-Calorie Grapefruit Vinaigrette (page 130) for dressing given; for vegetarian version, substitute ¾ pound tofu, Jarlsberg, Greek string cheese (separated) or Homemade Vegetable Protein (pages 35, 36) for the roast beef.

2 tablespoons wine vinegar
1 egg yolk
¼ cup salad oil
2 scallions sliced on diagonal
½ teaspoon salt or substitute
¼ teaspoon pepper
¼ cup mayonnaise
½ head leaf lettuce, cleaned, dried and chilled
¼ pound thinly sliced roast beef
¼ cup cooked macaroni shells
¼ pound sorrel
   Fake Bacon Bits (page 147), optional

GREEN DELI SALAD WITH SORREL

• To prepare dressing, place vinegar in bowl, add egg yolk and whisk until yolk dissolves in vinegar. Beat in oil, scallions, salt and pepper.
• Stir in mayonnaise. If dressing is too thick, thin with oil.
• Tear lettuce into salad bowl.
• Add the roast beef, macaroni and sorrel.
• Top with dressing, toss, garnish with Fake Bacon Bits if desired and serve.

2–3 servings.

Serve with: Toasted hardtack crackers.

Variations: Substitute fresh mint or watercress for sorrel; use leeks or shallots in place of scallions; use turkey breast instead of roast beef.

STUFFED GRAPE LEAVES WITH GARLIC DRESSING

1 cup cooked oats
1 cup cooked ground beef*
½ cup grated carrots
1 egg
¼ teaspoon salad oil
1¼ teaspoon dried parsley flakes
1¼ teaspoons sage
1¼ teaspoons dill
  Grated garlic, to taste
  Grated ginger, to taste
½ teaspoon salt or substitute
½ teaspoon soy sauce
¼ cup sunflower seeds
6 grape leaves, drained and rinsed
1 cup vegetable broth or water
1 clove garlic, sliced
1 teaspoon grated fresh ginger
¼ cup nut butter (peanut, almond, sesame)

• To prepare stuffing, stir together oats, ground beef and carrots with next 10 ingredients. Place a tablespoonful of the mixture in the center of each grape leaf. Fold in the sides, then fold over top and bottom to form a square package. Place the stuffed leaves, seam side down, in a steamer basket.

• In steamer kettle or pot, pour broth and add garlic and ginger. Set steamer basket in place, cover and bring to a boil. Steam for 20–30 minutes.

• Remove steamed stuffed leaves to platter and chill.

• Mix liquid remaining in steamer with nut butter and re-heat, stirring until thickened. Chill.

• Spoon chilled sauce over grape leaves and serve.

3–4 servings. Leftovers freeze well.

Serve with: Plain bread and Fancy Butter (page 155) and cheese cubes or pretzels.

Variations: Use steamed cabbage or Swiss chard leaves in place of grape leaves; use 2 cups cooked rice or millet in place of oats; use ½ cup grated raw sweet potato or shredded parsnips in place of carrots.

*Or use 2 cups cooked oats and no ground beef.

1 cup dry lentils
3 tablespoons red wine vinegar
2 tablespoons salad oil
1 teaspoon salt or substitute
Freshly ground pepper
1 cup slivered or cubed roast pork
6 large shallots, peeled and halved
2 fresh hot chili peppers, seeded and slivered
3 cups spinach leaves, chilled

LENTIL SALAD

• Wash lentils and drain. Place in saucepan with 3 cups water. Bring to a boil, reduce heat and cover pan. Simmer until tender, about 20 minutes.
• Rinse in a sieve or colander under cold running water to cool. Drain thoroughly.
• In a large bowl combine vinegar, oil, salt and ground pepper to taste; beat with a whisk. Add lentils, pork, shallots and chili peppers; mix thoroughly.
• Let stand at room temperature 1 hour, stirring occasionally. Serve over spinach leaves.

4 servings.

Serve with: Pumpkinseed Salad Wafers (page 153) or with toasted oyster crackers on top.

Variations: Splurge—skip the dressing above and use ¼ cup of balsamic vinegar instead (see page 120). For a vegetarian version, use 1 cup Homemade Vegetable Protein (pages 35, 36) in place of roast pork.

CHINESE PORK AND BEAN SALAD

¾ pound very fresh young string beans, trimmed, cut on the diagonal into ½-inch pieces
4 tablespoons finely chopped fresh coriander
1½ cups vinaigrette dressing of your choice
2 cups cooked, slivered roast pork
⅓ cup minced onion or scallion
White pepper
3½ cups shredded iceberg lettuce

• Blanch beans in salted, boiling water 3–4 minutes. Drain and refresh under cold running water so beans lose some heat but remain warm.
• Stir 2 tablespoons of the coriander into the vinaigrette.
• Toss the beans with ⅓ of the vinaigrette; set aside for 15 minutes.
• 30 minutes before serving, add roast pork, onion and remaining coriander to the string beans and toss to mix. Season with pepper. Moisten with another ¼ cup of vinaigrette.
• To serve, arrange lettuce on platter and top with pork and bean mixture. Serve with extra dressing on the side.

4 servings.

Serve with: Coriander Crackers (page 153) or warm pita bread on the side.

Variations: Substitute flat-leaf Italian parsley for fresh coriander; use 2 cups of chick-peas in place of pork for vegetarian version.

WHOLE MEAL CITRUS SALAD

 1 tablespoon lemon juice
¼ cup salad oil
½ teaspoon salt or substitute
⅛ teaspoon freshly ground pepper
 2 cups packed, shredded red or green cabbage
 2 medium oranges, peeled, pith removed and
    separated into segments
½ small leek, sliced thin (white part only) or 2
    scallions, chopped fine (¼ cup)
1½ cups cold roast pork or cold crumbled pork sausage
    patties
1½ cups torn spinach leaves
¼ cup croutons

• In salad bowl, blend lemon juice, oil, salt or substitute and pepper.
• Add cabbage, oranges, leek and pork. Toss to mix.
• Chill ½ hour. Serve over spinach. Sprinkle with croutons.

2–3 servings.

Serve with: Fruit-Filled Croissants (page 160) or sesame crackers.

Variations: Use romaine lettuce in place of spinach; tangerines or papaya in place of oranges; sprinkle with toasted wheat germ instead of croutons.

ONE POTATO, TWO POTATO SALAD

2 pounds cold boiled new potatoes, peeled and cut into 1-inch cubes
½ teaspoon turmeric
8 tablespoons vegetable oil
1½ cups onion, grated or chopped
1 to 2 green chilies, seeded and minced
1½ teaspoons cumin seed
2 to 3 teaspoons fresh lemon juice
12 slices cooked lean thick-sliced bacon (or 6 slices Canadian bacon), julienned
6 tablespoons plain or flavored mayonnaise (see pages 133–135)
   Salt or substitute
4 cups mixed light and dark greens

• Sprinkle potatoes with turmeric, toss to coat and set aside.
• In a large heavy skillet, heat 2 tablespoons of vegetable oil and sauté the onions over medium heat until they are soft and golden. Remove and set aside.
• Heat the remaining 6 tablespoons of oil in the skillet. When the oil is hot, add the turmeric-coated potatoes, turning and tossing them rapidly over medium-high heat. Lower the heat slightly and continue stir-frying the potatoes until they begin to brown. Add the sautéed onions, minced chilies and cumin seed and continue frying over medium heat, stirring constantly, until the potatoes are crunchy and the onions brown.
• Remove the skillet from the heat. When the potatoes have cooled to room temperature, add the lemon juice, bacon and mayonnaise. Mix well; add salt to taste.
• Transfer to a bowl, cover loosely and refrigerate at least one hour. Serve over greens.

4 servings.

Serve with: 20-Calorie Potato Shells (page 160) or salt-free corn chips.

Variations: Saving calories? Substitute 2 cups of cooked, peeled and chilled Jerusalem artichokes in place of potatoes.

½ pound asparagus, trimmed and cut into 2-inch
    pieces
1 pound Canadian bacon, sautéed and slivered
1 cup cooked peas (fresh or frozen)
2 tablespoons minced scallions
2 cups watercress or mâche
1 cup Boston lettuce

DRESSING:

3 tablespoons olive oil
½ cup buttermilk
1 tablespoon lemon juice
⅛ teaspoon salt or salt substitute
⅛ teaspoon fresh-cracked pepper
1 teaspoon curry powder
½ teaspoon cumin

CANADIAN BACON SALAD WITH CURRY DRESSING

• Steam asparagus until tender; drain well.
• Place bacon, asparagus and next 4 ingredients in a large salad bowl.
• Mix dressing, add to salad, toss and serve.

2 servings.

Serve with: Corn Chip Topping (page 145) or radish roses and chilled carrot curls.

Variations: Substitute Pecan Dressing (page 53) for dressing above; use flat-leafed parsley in place of cress; use artichoke hearts in place of asparagus.

B.L.T. PLUS

½ head iceberg lettuce, finely shredded
1 bunch watercress, washed, dried and stemmed
1 cup red or yellow cherry tomato halves
1 tablespoon fresh lemon juice
¼ pound mushrooms, thinly sliced
6 slices crisp cooked bacon, crumbled
4 tablespoons olive oil
2 tablespoons fresh lemon juice
1 clove garlic, mashed
½ teaspoon salt or substitute
¼ teaspoon freshly ground pepper
¼ teaspoon dry mustard
1 egg yolk
Wheat germ or a Salad Sprinkle (page 150) of your
   choice

• Place lettuce and watercress in salad bowl. Top with to-matoes. Sprinkle lemon juice over the mushrooms, add to bowl and top with crumbled bacon. Cover and chill.
• To prepare dressing, combine oil, lemon juice, garlic, salt, pepper and mustard. Mix well. Beat in the egg yolk. Chill.
• At serving time, pour dressing over salad and toss. Sprin-kle on wheat germ and serve.

2–3 servings.

Serve with: Garlic croutons (page 145) on top or 1-2-3 Melba Toast (page 151) on the side.

Variations: Substitute strips of Canadian bacon for reg-ular bacon; use broiled, crumbled tempeh (see page 47) in place of bacon for a vegetarian version; substitute Hurry-Up Thousand Island (page 120) for dressing given.

1 large or 2 small heads romaine
½ red onion, thinly sliced (optional)
  About 2 cups slightly stale Italian bread (preferably whole wheat), cut in 1-inch cubes
1 cup julienned strips of prosciutto
½ cup olive oil
¼ cup red wine vinegar
1 teaspoon dried basil or 2 teaspoons fresh
1 or 2 cloves garlic, minced or crushed
¾ teaspoon salt or substitute

FLORENTINE BREAD SALAD

• Tear thoroughly dried, chilled romaine leaves into bite-size pieces and place in bowl with onion, bread cubes and prosciutto.
• Place olive oil, vinegar, basil, garlic and salt in small bowl. Beat with whisk or fork until blended.
• Drizzle dressing over salad ingredients and toss until romaine is well coated and bread has soaked up most of the dressing. Chill before serving.

3 servings.

Serve with: Corn, potato or shrimp chips on the side.

Variations: Use 1 bunch watercress or radicchio for half the romaine; use sesame oil in place of olive oil and rye bread in place of Italian bread; substitute hot pickled Italian or jalapeño peppers for red onion; for a vegetarian version, use julienned strips of Swiss or Jarlsberg cheese in place of prosciutto.

HAM AND CHEESE COLESLAW

1 cup shredded Chinese cabbage
1 cup shredded red or green cabbage
½ cup ricotta cheese
¼ cup white wine vinegar
1 tablespoon heavy cream
1 teaspoon anchovy paste
1 teaspoon Dijon-style mustard
  Salt or substitute, to taste
  Freshly ground pepper, to taste
1 tablespoon minced fresh basil
1 teaspoon minced chives
2 tablespoons Homemade Capers (page 169), optional
1 cup slivered baked ham or prosciutto

• Combine shredded cabbages in large salad bowl.
• For dressing, puree the next 7 ingredients in a blender or food processor. Add to cabbage and toss.
• Stir in the basil, chives and capers (if desired).
• Top with slivered ham.

4–5 servings.

Serve with: Vegetable Crisps (page 155) or Cheesy Eggplant Sticks (page 152) or top with oyster crackers.

Variations: Substitute 1 cup mustard greens for the Chinese cabbage; add diced water chestnuts for extra crunch.

NEW POTATO SALAD

¼ cup red wine vinegar
1 teaspoon anchovy paste
1 teaspoon salt or substitute
½ teaspoon freshly ground pepper
¾ cup olive oil
1 pound freshly cooked small new potatoes, peeled
⅓ pound sliced salami, cut into ¼-inch strips
2 small red bell peppers, cut into thin slivers
¼ cup minced black or green olives
½ cup minced scallions
1 or more tablespoons poppy seeds, caraway seeds or Salad Sprinkles (see page 150) of your choice
1 cup pecan halves
2 cups fresh spinach leaves

• In a medium bowl, whisk vinegar, anchovy paste, salt and pepper until blended. Whisk in oil until smooth and creamy.
• Place warm potatoes in a large serving bowl and toss with the dressing until well coated. Add the salami, red peppers, olives and scallions and toss to mix. Sprinkle with poppy seeds, caraway seeds or Salad Sprinkles. Cover and chill several hours or overnight. Top with pecans and serve over fresh spinach.

4 servings.

Serve with: Cheese-sprinkled popcorn on the side.

Variations: Substitute 1 pound of water chestnuts for potatoes; for a vegetarian version, substitute ⅓ pound thinly sliced cheese for salami and use miso in place of anchovy paste.

SICHUAN VEAL SALAD

2½ cups cold, cooked and shredded veal
1 tablespoons hot Chinese mustard
1 tablespoon sesame seeds
2 ribs celery, sliced diagonally
3 green onions, sliced diagonally
1 small bunch Chinese parsley, chopped
1 tablespoon soy sauce
2 tablespoons salad oil
1 tablespoon sesame oil
¼ teaspoon ground ginger
3 cups shredded iceberg lettuce

• Combine veal with hot mustard and stir well to coat.
• Toast sesame seeds, sprinkling on cookie sheet and bake in a preheated 350° oven for 8 minutes until golden.
• Toss together seeds (reserve ½ teaspoon for garnish), celery, green onions, parsley (reserve one parsley sprig for garnish) and veal.
• Mix soy sauce, oils, ginger. Add to veal and mix. Arrange shredded lettuce on a large platter and mound veal salad on top. Garnish with sprig of parsley and toasted sesame seeds.

4 servings.

Serve with: Chinese Chips (page 148) or canned toasted chow mein noodles.

Variations: Use Italian flat-leaf parsley or fresh mint in place of Chinese parsley; use chopped cashews in place of sesame seeds.

HALF-A-MINUTE SALADS AND 30-SECOND DRESSINGS

Got a minute? That's all it takes to make salad or dressing. Here are lots of quick ways to keep salad on the menu for a month:

SALADS

• Spinach, leaf lettuce, young dandelion greens, radishes, snow peas and scallions, plus 1 tablespoon crushed fennel seed, oil and vinegar.

• Oak-tip or butterhead lettuce, basil and sliced pears (canned or fresh). Add lemon juice or lemon vinegar.

• Chopped mint, basil, parsley, cherry tomato halves, scallions, feta cheese. Dress with One-Minute Vinaigrette (page 119).

• Oak-tip lettuce, sesame seeds, grapefruit sections. Try True Blue Dressing (page 119) or a dash of raspberry vinegar.

• Chard or kale, sliced hard-boiled egg, chick-peas, Bibb lettuce, nasturtium blossoms. Toss with Fast French Dressing (page 119).

• Watercress (or Boston or Bibb lettuce and basil or tarragon), red onion rings, walnuts. Good with Fast Tamari Dressing (page 119).

• Any loose-leaf lettuce with fresh raspberries, sliced strawberries, whole blueberries and sprouts. Sprinkle with raspberry vinegar or with lime juice and sesame oil.

• One-Step Sesame Potato Salad: Cut 2½ cups leftover cooked potatoes into bite-sized pieces. Toss with 2 tablespoons toasted sesame seeds and 1 teaspoon crumbled dill. Bind with plain mayonnaise or Cashew Mayonnaise (page 119).

• Avocado, bean sprouts, tomato and lettuce. Bind with Hawaiian Mayonnaise (page 120).

• Avocado, shredded Cheddar cheese, chopped scallions and shredded lettuce. Dress with 1–2–3 Tahini (page 119).

• Turkey, avocado and alfalfa sprouts. Dress with Fast French (page 119) or Fast Tamari (page 119).

• Corned beef, onion slices and well-drained coleslaw. Top with 30-Second Russian Dressing (page 120).

• Sliced broiled chicken livers and bacon, thin slices onion, tomato and lettuce with One-Minute Vinaigrette (page 119).

• Sliced raw mushrooms and raw zucchini, tomato, chopped scallions. Toss with Fast French Dressing (page 119).

• Tomato, thin slices raw zucchini and alfalfa sprouts. Dress with raspberry vinegar.

• Tomato, marinated artichoke hearts, lettuce. Bind with Quick Curried Mayo (page 119).

• Feta cheese, sliced olives, tomatoes, alfalfa sprouts, fresh spinach leaves. Fast Fruit Dressing (page 119) on top.

• Shredded cabbage, shredded carrot, chopped scallions, bean sprouts and Orange 'n' Blue Dressing (page 119).

• Sliced hearts of palm, tomato, watercress, and 10-Calorie Dressing (page 119).

• Sliced cold (leftover) sweetbreads, yellow cherry tomatoes, shredded iceberg lettuce and One-Minute Vinaigrette (page 119).

• Parsley and Coconut Salad: Combine 3 cups chopped parsley, 2 cups shredded unsweetened coconut, juice of a lemon and salt or substitute. Good with One-Minute Vinaigrette (page 119).

• Self-Dressing Caesar Salad: Two cups romaine tossed with olive oil, crushed garlic cloves, salt or substitute, paprika, a coddled egg, lemon juice, anchovies, croutons and grated Parmesan cheese.

• French Carrot Toss: Combine 1 pound carrots, peeled and coarsely grated, 2 tablespoons chopped fresh parsley, ¼ cup olive oil or vegetable oil, ½ teaspoon salt and pepper to taste. Serve over spears of endive. Top with 30-Second Sprout/Soy Dressing (page 120).

• Beans Plus: Cold cooked beans, shredded romaine or radicchio and cubes of Swiss cheese. Mix with Tomato-Plus Dressing (page 120).

• Boston lettuce, cooked broccoli, sardines, dry-roasted peanuts. Toss with 10-Calorie Dressing (page 119).

• Raw spinach, canned onion rings, shredded beets and pimientos. Toss with peanut oil and lemon juice.

• Any pale lettuce plus any dark green. Sprinkle with any vinaigrette and top with croutons.

• 30-Second Health Salad: Alfalfa or mung sprouts, watercress, sunflower seeds, grated carrot. Dress with lime juice and safflower oil.

• Quick Chef's Salad: Any shredded cabbage, torn greens, slivered cheese and cubed meat with 1 sliced egg, oil and vinegar.

• Swiss chard, Swiss cheese, diced apple, shredded parsnips. True Blue Dressing (page 119) on top.

DRESSINGS

• Fast Tamari Dressing: Place ⅛ teaspoon cayenne, ¼ teaspoon dry mustard, 1 teaspoon tamari, ½ clove garlic and juice of ½ lemon in blender. Blend 10 seconds to combine. With blender running, slowly add ⅓ cup vegetable oil. Use over any leaf lettuces.

• Fast French Dressing: Place 1 raw egg yolk, ½ teaspoon paprika, pinch dry mustard, 1 tablespoon honey and ½ cup red vinegar in blender. Process 30 seconds. Add ¾ cup sunflower oil in a slow stream until dressing thickens. Use on any mixed green or fruit salad.

• Quick Curried Mayo: In a small saucepan combine 2 tablespoons boiling water or chicken broth and 1 teaspoon curry powder. Cook gently over low heat a few seconds. Fold in ⅔ cup mayonnaise. Cool.

• Orange 'n' Blue Dressing: Combine 1 teaspoon fresh grated orange peel, 2 tablespoons fresh orange juice, 1 cup plain yogurt, ½ cup mayonnaise, 2 tablespoons crumbled blue cheese and ¼ teaspoon salt or substitute.

• Fast Fruit Dressing: Liquefy in blender pulp of ½ lemon, juice of 2 oranges, 1 avocado, 1 papaya, pinch of salt or substitute.

• 1-2-3 Tahini: Mix 3 parts tahini with 1 part soy sauce. Add grated onion. Thin with lemon juice, yogurt or tomato juice.

• 10-Calorie Dressing: Combine 1 pound pot cheese or small curd cottage cheese with 1 clove garlic, mashed, and 1 tablespoon chopped parsley. Add salt or substitute to taste and skim milk to thin. 10 calories a tablespoon.

• Roquefort on the Quick: Process 2 ounces room-temperature Roquefort cheese with ½ cup milk, 1 tablespoon sour cream and the juice of 1 lemon in blender until smooth.

• True Blue Dressing: ½ cup heavy cream, ⅓ cup crumbled French blue or Roquefort cheese and 2 tablespoons mayonnaise. Whip with a wire whisk to desired consistency.

• One-Minute Vinaigrette: 3 cloves garlic, crushed (or garlic to taste), 1 cup olive or peanut oil, ¼ cup sherry vinegar or white wine vinegar, 1 teaspoon salt or substitute, 1 tablespoon Dijon-style mustard, ¼ teaspoon freshly ground pepper and ¼ cup parsley sprigs. Process in blender or food processor 30 seconds, or until completely blended.

• Cashew Mayo: In a blender or food processor, process 1 cup raw cashews with 1 cup chopped celery. Add plain yogurt or sour cream as needed to reach the consistency of mayonnaise.

• 30-Second Indonesian: Combine 3 thinly sliced green chilies, 3 cloves minced garlic, ½ cup roasted peanuts, 3 tablespoons soy sauce, 3 tablespoons lemon juice and 1 tablespoon honey in a blender. Blend into a smooth, thick sauce. (This is traditionally made by pounding the ingredients together in a mortar.)

• 30-Second Sprout/Soy Dressing: Mix 1 tablespoon rice wine vinegar or apple cider vinegar, 1 tablespoon soy sauce, 1 teaspoon ground ginger, 2 tablespoons sliced scallions and ¼ cup fresh bean sprouts (mung, lentil, chick-pea). Toss to blend.

• Flash Fruit Dressing: Combine 3 tablespoons orange juice, 2 tablespoons honey, 1 tablespoon lemon juice and 1 tablespoon minced fresh mint with 1 cup plain yogurt. Add chopped seedless grapes to taste.

• Creamy Sprout Dressing: Process in blender 1 cup alfalfa sprouts, 1 cup diced pineapple, ¼ cup toasted sesame seeds. Good on slaws.

• O.J. Mayo: Beat 1 egg yolk and ½ cup orange juice into 2 cups any plain mayonnaise.

• 30-Second Russian Dressing: Add 3 tablespoons of chili sauce to 1 cup of plain mayonnaise. Optional: Add 1 teaspoon prepared horseradish.

• Hurry-Up Thousand Island: Add 2 tablespoons chili sauce to 1 cup mayo along with 1 tablespoon chopped sweet pepper and 1 teaspoon chives.

• If you have one bottle of good white wine vinegar, you've got nine dressings you didn't know about. Add 1 to 2 cups of any of the following fresh herbs to 1 quart white wine vinegar (the longer they steep, the better they taste): fresh violets (use for fruit salads); chives (regular or garlic); blue borage flowers; tarragon (use for fish or meat); savory or rosemary (use for poultry salads); marjoram or dill (use for poultry salads); coriander seeds (use for fruit salads); basil; orange-mint or lemon-mint leaves.

• The simplest salad dressing of all? A splash of Italy's famous extra-potent gourmet balsamic vinegar. (If you can't find it locally, see "Mail Order Sources.") Try it on fresh whole strawberries with minced sorrel.

• Tomato Plus: Blend 2 parts diced tomato with 1 part diced pineapple. Optional: add green olive oil or finely diced avocado.

• Hawaiian Mayonnaise: Blend fresh coconut milk, avocado, 1 apple, ½ cup fresh shredded coconut.

ALL DRESSED UP

Salad Dressing Ingredients

"A spendthrift for oil, a miser for vinegar, a counselor for salt and a madman to stir it all up," goes an old Spanish proverb. Not a bad rule of thumb for the occasional salad maker. But if you go in for salads often, it leaves a lot unsaid. And if your salads aren't always on the best-dressed lists, here are a few suggestions.

Dressings on salads serve two purposes: They bind ingredients and increase the food value. Light vinaigrette dressings go well with delicate greens. Strongly flavored or creamy dressings are good for greens such as iceberg or romaine. Dressings made with mayonnaise, sour cream or yogurt can be used for seafood, meat or vegetable salads. But keep it simple and season it right. Use just enough to coat ingredients and if you want to avoid wilted greens, add at the very last minute before serving.

The precise quantities of oil and vinegar to be used in a salad dressing depend on individual taste and the type of salad involved. The most frequently recommended proportion is 3 parts oil to 1 part vinegar or lemon juice. But salads that contain a slightly fatty or oily ingredient—roast duck, for example—may call for a bit more acid; and those that contain an acidic ingredient, such as a fruit, may need less. Taste and make adjustments.

Proportions vary according to the degree of acidity of the vinegar you use. Vinegars vary in acidic strength, from mild rice vinegars to sturdy grape wine vinegars, and lemon juice can vary, too. If you add prepared mustard to a standard dressing, that too will change its acid nature.

Seafood salads are among the finest of summer salads, but use a light hand. A tablespoon of mustard and a tablespoon of vinegar and lemon juice combined is the amount of acid needed for slightly less than six tablespoons of oil. Experiment.

Try mashing garlic with the pepper and salt before adding it to your dressing.

Add tomatoes last to prevent a soggy salad. The same goes for any other juicy fruit or vegetable.

Fresh herbs beat dried. Use them whenever possible.

Oil. Which one to invest in? Go first class. Oil, after all, carries the flavor in the dressing and therefore is the heart and soul of the salad. Many salad lovers consider olive oil tops, but be aware that budget brands labeled "100 percent imported" lack the intense flavor of more expensive brands and, therefore, are not really a bargain. Olive oil comes from green olives pressed in a vat; the best of the many pressings or grades is the first, called "extra-virgin." Next in price and quality is "virgin." I prefer the clear, amber olive oils from France, and then the slightly heavier, dark green Italian fruity ones. In third place in my book are the good but strong-flavored Spanish oils. For taste and economy, olive oil may be blended with another salad oil at home to make a less costly all-purpose dressing. Keep small amounts of other special oils on hand to keep salads interesting—walnut, hazelnut, avocado, grape seed, safflower and sesame oil can be found in health food stores and gourmet food shops. Buy in small amounts and keep refrigerated; oils are rapid spoilers. Corn and peanut oil are readily available in any supermarket. So is the ubiquitous safflower oil, made from a plant which grows in warm climates such as India, southern France and the Middle East. The flowers which are orange, yellow and red are used to color everything from fabrics to face creams. It's the seeds that are pressed to make safflower oil—a neutral-tasting oil—and it's richer in healthy polyunsaturated fats than any others.

Vinegar. Obtained by the fermentation of anything from an apple to a grain of rice. Although the word comes from French *vin aigre,* literally "sour wine," age alone will not turn wine into vinegar. (See footnote on page 173 for how to make your own wine vinegar.) The best vinegars for most salads are wine vinegars—red is the most common; white, rosé and sherry are other possibilities. But the true-bluest of vinegars is Italy's balsamic vinegar. It's rich and dark and can even be used with nothing else but oil to dress a salad. Other vinegars to use to beat the salad blues include malt vinegar (British), rice-wine vinegar (Oriental), and vinegars flavored with herbs, spices, fruits, even flowers and weeds. Whatever you use, don't overdo it. Too much vinegar sets you up for a watery acid dressing that you'll wind up throwing out. Always buy good vinegars, clear in color, with a pronounced acid taste. (See pages 173, 174 for homemade flavored vinegars.)

Lemon juice. Like vinegar, lemon adds an acid note to a salad dressing, but a lighter one. It can be interchanged with vinegar in any salad dressing but is especially appropriate in fruit salads and over delicate greens, and when wine is on your menu. Lemon juice also prevents cut fruits such as apples and bananas from darkening after cutting. Look for firm yellow lemons, heavy for their size with no green tinges. Squeeze just before using to prevent loss of flavor and vitamin C. If you're fresh out of lemons, try lime or grapefruit juice. For a lemony taste and fragrance with none of the acidity, try a lemony herb—lemon thyme, lemon balm, lemon verbena or lemon grass. Sorrel is the opposite—lemony sour, without a lemon fragrance. Lemon rind, fresh or dried, is also a substitute for lemon juice.

Mustard. Unique to mustard among salad spices is its lack of aroma when dry. Mustard should be moistened and allowed to sit for ten minutes to develop its sharp flavor: The liquid sets enzymes in action and an acid such as lemon juice, vinegar, or wine will help retain the flavor.

Hot, semi-mild and mild prepared mustards each require a different kind of seed. French and German mustards use the more pungent black or brown seeds, while yellow American mustards are usually based on milk yellow or white seeds. Once ground, the seeds are mixed with wine, vinegar or water, and then spices are added to produce a dark yellow to light olive brown mustard.

When adding it to a salad or dressing, use either dry or Dijon-style mustard. Salad type dictates amount: Use less for delicate tossed greens, more for the stick-to-your-ribs type salads that include meats, seafood or poultry. (Recipes for homemade mustards are on pages 171–172).

Low-Sodium Seasonings

Most versions of most salad dressings, whether commercial or homemade, contain salt, often too much. If you'd like to skip salt or reduce it, here are some off-the-shelf salt substitutes you can buy or make at home:

Dry Mustard. Provides bite. Try buying whole mustard seeds and freshly grinding your own.

Ginger. Fresh, not powdered, for zing in salads. Most potent part: the juice. Use a garlic press to extract the juice from a piece of ginger (and juice a garlic clove while you're at it. Garlic and ginger are perfect partners).

Horseradish. You can buy prepared horseradish refrigerated in jars, the fresh root or horseradish powder (Oriental food section of supermarkets).

Lemon Peel. Grate, dry and freeze your own supply. Fresh lemons and bottled lemon juice are shelf essentials, too.

Low- or No-Sodium Soup Cubes or Powder. These nutritious vegetable and soybean protein-based seasonings are low in salt and free of MSG.

Dried Mushrooms or Mushroom Flakes. When ground with vegetable flakes, they give a meatlike texture, appearance and flavor to meat-free salads.

Herbs. Oregano, savory, thyme, marjoram, basil, dill and especially French tarragon. Buy a quality brand if you don't grow and dry your own.

Cayenne. A little of this powdered red pepper adds a lot of bite.

Paprika. A salt and pepper substitute, but only the fresh Hungarian variety has any character.

Pickling Spices, Fines Herbes, Poultry Seasoning, Crab or Shrimp Boil Seasoning. Use as is or in combination with other salt-substitute seasonings. Spices that are sold whole should be ground before using.

Seeds. Try caraway, sesame, pumpkin, sunflower, dill, or the healthier-than-poppy-seed substitute, chia seed. The list is endless. To intensify taste, toast seeds in a dry skillet before grinding.

Sugar. Use a pinch in place of MSG to intensify flavor in dressings.

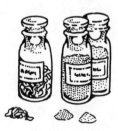

In addition to salt and its alternatives, here are other ingredients a salad-maker's pantry should stock:*

- Basil
- Bay leaves
- Caraway seeds
- Cayenne
- Celery leaves and seeds
- Chervil
- Chives
- Curry powder (a blend of spices—available medium hot, extra hot, Malaysian)
- Dillweed and dill seeds
- Dried garlic and onion flakes†
- Ginger
- Kelp powder, dulse flakes†
- Marjoram††
- Mustard powder†
- Oregano†
- Paprika
- Parsley††
- Poppy seeds
- Rosemary
- Sage
- Savory
- Sesame Seeds
- Tarragon††
- Thyme
- Turmeric

Basic Herbs, Spices and Seeds Not To Be Without

*One tablespoon of fresh herbs equals ⅓–½ teaspoon dried.
†Salt substitute.
††Good choice for the indoor salad gardener (see page 27).

Not So Basic Health Spices To Try From Time To Time

- Borage
- Cassia
- Carnation Petals (edible flower buds and petals)
- Burnet (cucumber-flavored)
- Catnip (or cat mint)
- Chamomile
- Chinese star anise (spicy, peppery) or Chinese 5-spice powder
- Cinnamon
- Coriander (fragrant, fruity)
- Cumin
- Fennel and aniseed (licorice-like)
- Geranium and nasturtium leaves and flowers (peppery)
- Hibiscus
- Horseradish powder
- Hyssop
- Lemon balm or lemon grass
- Lovage
- Pineapple mint

How To Make the Perfect Salad Dressing

A salad isn't a salad until it's all dressed up. The basics aren't hard to master, and the possibilities unlimited.

As a reference point, here are five of the basic formulas:

- Basic Vinaigrette—oil and acid vinegar or lemon juice and seasoning.

- Basic French—same as vinaigrette with dry mustard and paprika.

- Basic Mayonnaise—also known as old fashioned Oil-Egg-and-Vinegar.

- Basic Russian—mayonnaise, chili sauce and onion with or without olives and pickles.

- Basic Thousand Island—mayonnaise, chili sauce and red or green pepper, olive or pickles.

VINAIGRETTE AND OTHER THIN DRESSINGS

• Whisk together 2 tablespoons vinegar or lemon juice, ½ teaspoon salt or substitute and freshly ground pepper to taste.
• Gradually beat in 6 to 8 tablespoons olive oil or other salad oil. Mix well. For a sharper dressing add a pinch of dry mustard or Dijon-style mustard to the vinegar before adding oil.
• Mix the dressing immediately before serving.

Makes ½ cup

BASIC FRENCH DRESSING OR VINAIGRETTE

5 VARIATIONS

Chiffonade French Dressing: To ½ cup Basic French Dressing add 2 hard-boiled eggs, finely chopped; 1 tablespoon each of finely chopped pickled beets and green olives; and 1 teaspoon each of grated onion and chopped parsley. Makes about 1 cup.

Curried French Dressing: To ½ cup Basic French Dressing add 2 teaspoons finely chopped shallots or scallions and ½ teaspoon curry powder. Makes about ½ cup.

Hot French Dressing: Heat 1 cup Basic French Dressing to the boiling point, add 2 hard-boiled eggs, chopped, 1 tablespoon each of finely chopped parsley, green celery leaves and chives; 1 teaspoon dry mustard; and ½ teaspoon Worcestershire sauce. Beat well. Serve hot over a salad of asparagus, broccoli, cauliflower or cabbage. Makes about 1½ cups.

Sesame Seed French Dressing: Sauté 1 clove garlic, finely chopped, and 1 teaspoon sesame seeds in ½ cup olive oil until browned. Let mixture cool. Mix 2 tablespoons red wine vinegar with ¼ teaspoon salt or substitute and freshly ground pepper to taste, and ½ teaspoon paprika (optional). Add sesame seed mixture to the vinegar and blend well. Chill before serving. Makes about ½ cup.

Cumberland French Dressing: With a fork beat together 3 tablespoons lemon juice, 1 tablespoon each of red currant jelly and heavy cream, and ½ teaspoon salt or substitute. Gradually beat in ½ cup olive oil. Mix the dressing well and add ⅛ teaspoon grated lemon rind and freshly ground pepper to taste. This is excellent with pork, game and poultry salads. Makes about ½ cup.

LIME VINAIGRETTE

1 small clove garlic, crushed
½ teaspoon salt or substitute
   Freshly ground pepper, to taste
¼ teaspoon Dijon-style mustard
2 to 2½ tablespoons lime juice
½ to ¾ cup olive oil

• Mash garlic and salt to a paste in a small bowl using the back of a spoon. Add pepper, mustard and lime juice and blend.
• Gradually whisk in olive oil until mixture is smooth and thick. Taste; add more juice or oil if necessary.

Enough to dress 4 whole meal salads.

Variation: To make Lime Liqueur Vinaigrette, add 1 tablespoon of a fruit-flavored liqueur, such as melon, to Lime Vinaigrette, above, when you add the mustard.

WALNUT VINAIGRETTE

½ cup walnut oil
¼ cup peanut or safflower oil
¼ cup raspberry vinegar, or to taste
   Salt
   Freshly ground pepper

• Combine the oils and vinegar in a small bowl. Blend well and season with salt and pepper to taste.

LOW-CALORIE GRAPEFRUIT VINAIGRETTE (only 10 calories a tablespoon)

½ cup fresh grapefruit juice
¼ cup distilled white vinegar
2 tablespoons water
½ teaspoon finely minced garlic
½ teaspoon chopped fresh basil
¼ teaspoon chopped fresh thyme
¼ teaspoon chopped fresh parsley
¼ teaspoon freshly ground pepper

• Whisk all ingredients together in a bowl or shake in a jar with a tight-fitting lid to mix.
• Refrigerate, covered, until ready to use.

Makes ¾ cup.

Note: More recipes for vinaigrette dressing can be found in "30-Second-Dressings" (page 119).

¼ cup lemon juice
¼ cup cider vinegar
¼ cup unsweetened apple juice
½ teaspoon dry mustard
½ teaspoon onion powder
½ teaspoon garlic powder
½ teaspoon paprika
½ teaspoon oregano
⅛ teaspoon thyme
⅛ teaspoon rosemary

HERBED OIL-FREE ITALIAN DRESSING

• Put all ingredients in a blender and blend well. Refrigerate overnight or longer before using.

Makes ¾ cup.

2 cups water
1 medium onion, chopped
1 medium cucumber, chopped
½ green pepper, chopped (optional)
2 cups vinegar (cider, wine or rice)
  Juice and pulp of 2 lemons
½ teaspoon garlic powder
½ teaspoon freshly ground pepper
1 teaspoon ground celery seed
1 teaspoon dill
3 tablespoons minced parsley

TANGY OIL-FREE GARDEN DRESSING

• In a blender, mix the first 4 ingredients together until vegetables are finely chopped. Add remaining ingredients and blend well until mixed. Chill.

Makes about 5½ cups.

Variation: To make Tomato French Dressing, use 1 cup tomato juice in place of 1 cup water.

½ cup sunflower seeds
½ teaspoon sea salt or substitute
¾ cup cold water
1 cup sunflower oil

SUNFLOWER DRESSING

• Process the seeds with the salt and water in a blender. When finely ground, slowly blend in the oil.
• Chill. Toss with any mixed greens.

Makes about 2 cups.

Variations: Substitute poppy seeds or oven-roasted pomegranate or papaya seeds for the sunflower seeds.

PAPAYA SEED SALAD DRESSING

¾ cup honey
1 teaspoon salt or substitute
1 teaspoon dry mustard
¾ cup cider vinegar
1 cup any bland oil
1 small onion
3 tablespoons papaya seeds (fresh or dried)

• Process all ingredients in a blender and refrigerate. Good over fruit or vegetable salads or with plain tossed greens.

Makes about 2½ cups.

Variations: Substitute poppy, caraway or pomegranate seeds for the peppery-flavored papaya seeds.

TAHINI SALAD DRESSING

½ cup tahini (sesame paste)
¼ cup olive oil
½ teaspoon salt or substitute
2 tablespoons lime juice
½ cup water
2 pinches dried thyme or tarragon

• Mix tahini with oil and salt, add lime juice and mix again.
• Add water, a few spoonfuls at a time, mixing thoroughly until smooth. Add thyme; mix well. Let dressing stand 20 minutes or more for flavors to develop before serving.

Makes 1¼ cups.

Note: This is an excellent protein-rich dressing for dark green salads, pasta and grain salads.

MAYONNAISE AND OTHER THICK DRESSINGS

The best mayonnaise is not only homemade, it's hand-made. Like to try your hand? Get out your whisk.

• Break 3 egg yolks (at room temperature) into a 2½-quart bowl. With a wire whisk, beat for several minutes, until pale and thick.
• Beat in ½ teaspoon Dijon-style mustard, ½ teaspoon salt and ½ tablespoon wine vinegar or lemon juice.
• Beat half a minute more, then start adding, by dribbles, ½ cup of top quality salad oil, olive oil or combination of the two. Beat constantly until oil has been absorbed and dressing thickens into mayonnaise.
• Add an additional 1½ cups oil by the tablespoon, beating to incorporate each addition. If sauce thickens too much, thin with drops of lemon juice or vinegar.
• Season with white pepper, more lemon juice or vinegar and salt or substitute to taste.

Makes 2 cups.

Tips: Mayonnaise too oily? Too thin? Curdled? Whip together ½ tablespoon prepared mustard and 1 tablespoon of the mayo. After they combine, add to the remaining mayonnaise drop by drop.

Foolproof mayonnaise when you're pressed for time? Use your food processor to mix.

HANDMADE MAYONNAISE

1 square or 4 ounces of tofu, drained
2 to 3 tablespoons lemon or lime juice
2 tablespoons salad oil
1 to 2 teaspoons soy sauce
    Freshly ground black pepper
    Fresh chopped parsley or coriander leaves, to taste
    (optional)

• Combine all ingredients in a food processor or blender and puree until smooth, or fork-mash to desired consistency.

Makes ½ cup.

EGG-FREE MAYONNAISE

Variations: To reduce fat and calories, replace the tofu with an equal amount of uncreamed cottage cheese, farmer's or hoop cheese, or drained plain yogurt.

WATERCRESS MAYONNAISE

1 egg yolk, at room temperature
1 tablespoon hot mustard
1 tablespoon vinegar
  Salt or substitute, to taste
  Freshly ground pepper, to taste
1 cup salad oil
½ bunch watercress, cleaned and minced

• Place egg yolk in a mixing bowl with mustard, vinegar, salt and pepper. Beat the mixture with a wire whisk to blend, then continue to whisk while adding the oil—a few drops at a time at first, then in a slow drizzle.
• When all the oil is incorporated, mix in the watercress and adjust seasoning.

Makes ¾ cup.

CALORIE-REDUCED MAYONNAISE #1 (fruity)

6 ounces low fat cream cheese (or Neufchâtel)
½ cup plain yogurt
½ cup small curd cottage cheese
½ cup orange juice
1 teaspoon grated orange rind
1 teaspoon honey (optional)

• Soften cream cheese at room temperature and mash with a fork. Blend in remaining ingredients.
• Chill and serve with fruit salads or use (omit honey) to make coleslaw.

Makes 2 cups.

Variations: To reduce calories even more, use farmer's cheese or hoop cheese in place of cottage cheese and use papaya juice in place of orange.

CALORIE-REDUCED MAYONNAISE #2 (spicy)

¾ cup small curd cottage cheese
2 teaspoons lemon juice
¼ teaspoon dry mustard
¼ teaspoon cayenne or Tabasco
¾ cup plain low fat yogurt

• Blend all ingredients except yogurt in a food processor or blender. Fold in the yogurt by hand.
• Chill and serve on vegetable salads or as a sandwich spread, or use to make coleslaw.

Makes 1½ cups.

1 medium tomato
1 teaspoon safflower oil
2 teaspoons minced chives, tarragon or Italian parsley
1 small or ½ medium ripe avocado, peeled and pitted

• Peel and seed tomato, place in blender or food processor, add oil and herb and blend well. Add avocado and process until creamy.

About ½ cup.

GREEN MOCK MAYONNAISE #1

1 cup sour cream
¼ cup plain yogurt
1 cup raw spinach
½ small onion, chopped
½ teaspoon honey (optional)
¾ teaspoon salt or substitute
¼ teaspoon ground ginger
1 teaspoon dried dill seed or dillweed

• Mix all ingredients in a blender of food processor until smooth.

Makes 1½ cups.

Variation: Use watercress in place of spinach.

GREEN MOCK MAYONNAISE #2

1 medium cucumber, peeled, seeded and cubed
1 small bunch parsley
1 teaspoon safflower oil
2 teaspoons salt or substitute
¼ cup cashews

• Place cucumber and parsley in blender or food processor. Add oil and salt and blend. Add cashews; blend to mayonnaise consistency.

About 1 cup.

GREEN MOCK MAYONNAISE #3

MOCK SOUR CREAM #1

1 cup filberts (hazelnuts), toasted and skinned
½ cup sesame seeds
Warm water, as needed

• Grind together nuts and seeds in a coffee mill or nut grinder until fine.
• In a blender or bowl, add enough water to the ground mixture to achieve the consistency of heavy cream.
• Cover and allow to stand 8–15 hours in a warm kitchen (70° to 80°F) until it sours slightly and thickens to a yogurt-like consistency. Use on fruits and vegetable salads; makes a good chip dip, too.

Makes 1¼ cups.

MOCK SOUR CREAM #2

1 cup small curd cottage cheese
1 envelope dry onion soup mix
½ lemon, peeled, seeded and thinly sliced
½ cucumber, peeled, seeded and thinly sliced
2 tablespoons milk

• Put all ingredients in a blender and blend at medium speed until completely smooth (about 5 minutes). Especially good over any plain tossed salad.

About 1½ cups.

THICK AND CREAMY MUSTARD DRESSING

4 tablespoons Dijon-style mustard
6 tablespoons mayonnaise
3 cloves garlic, smashed or put through a garlic press
1 teaspoon red wine vinegar

• In a small bowl, mix everything together. Taste and add a little more vinegar if desired.

Dresses 4 salads.

Yogurt and whipped tofu are more than good low-calorie mayonnaise alternatives; they're the starting point for many light, low-calorie salad dressings. Here are eight easy-to-prepare ideas to get you started.

- Blend ¾ cup plain yogurt with 1 ounce crumbled blue cheese.

- Blend yogurt with a piece of peeled cucumber, chopped scallion, a small clove of minced garlic (optional), lemon juice and a sprinkle of dill, with or without a pinch of sugar.*

- Blend ⅔ cup yogurt with 2 tablespoons capers, a dash of chili powder and lemon juice to taste.

- Combine yogurt with lemon juice, a bit of honey and dill or curry powder to taste.

- Blend one square of tofu, 1 tablespoon lemon juice or vinegar, 1 teaspoon soy sauce, garlic and dill to taste.

- Follow preceding recipe, but omit dill and substitute paprika and lemon peel to taste.

- Follow tofu recipe above, but add 2 slices avocado and 1 tablespoon minced scallion in place of soy, garlic and dill.

- For a triple-cheese dressing, blend 1 cup tofu with ½ cup yogurt and 1 ounce crumbled Cheddar or feta cheese.

BASIC YOGURT AND TOFU DRESSINGS

1 ripe papaya, peeled and seeded
1 cup mayonnaise
2 tablespoons honey
½ teaspoon powdered ginger
Salt or substitute to taste

- Cut papaya into cubes and place in blender or food processor, add remaining ingredients and blend until smooth. Delicious on fresh fruit salads or sliced avocados.

2 cups.

JUICY FRUIT SALAD DRESSING

*What's sugar doing in a low-calorie salad dressing? Enhancing flavors, in place of MSG. Adding ground pepper to a fruity dressing has the same flavor-enhancing effect.

RED, WHITE AND BLUE PEPPER AND CHEESE SALAD DRESSING

1   egg
¼   cup chopped onion
1   teaspoon minced garlic
2   cups vegetable or olive oil
½   cup plain yogurt or buttermilk
½   teaspoon freshly ground pepper
2   teaspoons salt or substitute
½   teaspoon cayenne
½   pound blue cheese, coarsely crumbled

• In a food processor or blender, combine egg, onion and garlic and process a few seconds, until well mixed.
• With machine still running, add oil in a thin, steady stream. Next add yogurt, pepper, salt and cayenne. Process 30 seconds more until mixed (push down sides once with spatula).
• Transfer mixture to a large bowl and stir in cheese with a wire whisk. Cheese will be somewhat lumpy. Refrigerate. Use over any vegetable salad.

Makes 4 cups.

Variations: Substitute 1 cup slivered regular or low-salt Jarlsberg, Swiss or Jack for the blue cheese.

Uses for Leftover Salad Dressing

What to do with what's left. Here are ten good uses for good-to-the-last-drop dressings.

USE THIN DRESSINGS:

• As sauces for hot cooked vegetables.

• As appetizer dips for vegetables, meatballs and shrimp.

• As flavor enhancers for casseroles and one-dish dinners.

• As brush-and-broil sauces for meat, chicken, hamburgers and meatless patties.

• As a brush-and-bake spread on thick slices of French or Italian bread.

USE THICK DRESSINGS:

• As sauces for vegetables, meats, open-faced sandwiches.

• As dips for crisp fresh vegetables, fruit sticks and chips.

• As flavor bases for casseroles and one-dish dinners.

• As ingredient binders for sandwich fillings.

• As baste-and-bake coatings: Baste your fish, meat or fowl in the dressing, then roll in crumbs or grated cheese and bake.

How To Read a Salad Dressing Label

America loves salad dressings almost as much as its leafy greens. Maybe more. Sales of bottled dressings alone have increased 1200 percent in the last decade. We consume 400 million gallons of store-bought dressings a year, not all of it top quality or healthy. Would you suspect that dressing your greens with just 2 tablespoons of Wishbone dressing adds more fat and almost as much salt to your diet as a McDonald's cheeseburger?

For instance, here's what you get per tablespoon from eight best-selling brands of Italian dressing:

BRANDS	CALORIES	FAT (g)	POLY-UNSATURATED FAT (g)	SODIUM (mg)	ADDED COLOR
REGULAR					
Kraft	80	8	5	240	none
Wishbone	80	8	5	284	natural
Seven Seas	70	7	3	400	artificial
REDUCED CALORIE					
Kraft	6	0	0	220	artificial
Wishbone	30	3	2	192	natural
Walden Farms*	9	1	1	300	none
NO OIL					
Kraft*	4	0	0	220	none
Herb Magic	4	0	0	NA	none

*Preservative free.

And here's the scoreboard for French, Blue Cheese and Russian:

	CALORIES	FAT (g)
Blue Cheese		
Regular	80	8
Reduced Calorie	14	1
Thousand Island or French		
Regular	60	6
Reduced Calorie	25	2
Russian		
Regular	60	5
Reduced Calorie	25	1

What's a health-minded salad fancier to do? Know what's in store before she gets to the store. Here's what the typical commercial salad dressing supplies:

1. *Calories.* One tablespoon contains 60 to 80 calories— as much as a slice of bread. Two tablespoons are the caloric equivalent of a scoop of ice cream or a slice of pizza.

2. *Fat.* Store-bought salad dressings are diet busters because 80 to 95 percent of the calories come from fat. It's unsaturated fat so it doesn't hike blood cholesterol levels or increase your risk of heart disease, but the National Cancer Institute cautions against consumption of *all* fats to reduce your risk of breast and bowel cancer.

3. *Sugar and Salt.* Ninety-nine percent of all salad dressings are high scorers here. Italian varieties are highest in sodium (150–400 milligrams per tablespoon), while Russian, French and Thousand Island dressings are highest in sugar. Wishbone Russian dressing contains almost two teaspoons of sugar per tablespoon, twice as much as a tablespoon of chocolate pudding.

4. *Additives.* Three types of additives commonly appear in dressings: emulsifiers, preservatives and coloring. The emulsifiers (xanthum gum, propylene glycol alginate, hydroxypropylmethyl cellulose, etc.) are derived from microorganisms, seaweed or starch, which pose

no health risk. But most artificial colors used are synthetic dyes derived from coal tar, several of which are suspected of causing organ damage and cancer. Look for brands that use natural colors—such as beet juice, carotene or annatto (i.e., Kraft Regular Italian), or none at all (no-oil Herb Magic).

5. *Reduced Calories.* Removing 60 to 100 percent of the oil is how calories are cut. Low-calorie dressings vary substantially in calorie and fat content. Some contain only six calories per tablespoon, others 30. And some brands only seem lower because they reduce the serving size from 1 tablespoon to 1 teaspoon. Dressings with no oil contain fewer than 10 calories per tablespoon and may be preservative-free and low in sodium as well.

DESCRIPTIVE LABEL TERMS

"Low-calorie": No more than 40 calories per serving (0.4 calories per gram).

"Reduced-calorie": At least ⅓ fewer calories per serving than regular. According to law, if, for example, most regular Italian salad dressings have 100 calories per serving, the reduced-calorie equivalent can have no more than 67.

"Sugar-free" and "no sugar added": No sugar, sucrose, dextrose, fructose, glucose, honey, molasses or syrup. But substitute sweeteners such as sorbitol, mannitol, or xylitol (which are almost as high in calories) are permitted. So is the controversial new low-calorie sweetener aspartame and the potentially hazardous calorie-free saccharin.

"Lite" and "Light": Maybe fewer calories than regular versions, maybe not. Compare actual numbers.

TIPS

How can you get first-rate when you buy second best?

Be wary of descriptions. "Original," for example, does not mean the ingredients are those in the recipe as originally conceived; any more than "extra rich" guarantees you extra cream, eggs or oil. And "country style" doesn't mean the ingredients are farm-fresh, either.

Avoid products with artificial flavorings, color and more than one source of sugar or salt (this includes MSG and any ingredient with "sodium" as a prefix).

Remember, "flavor enhancers" often add an unpleasant aftertaste to a dressing.

Private-label dressings (carrying the name of a well-known restaurant or a prestigious market or herb producer) are often very good. But check the ingredient list before you buy. Gourmet food shops, cheese stores, quality delicatessens that cater and mail order firms are good sources.

Chilled-before-you-buy-them dressings sold in produce departments next to the greens they go with are usually a healthy choice.

Low-calorie dressings may prove to be inordinately high in sodium and additives. Why not try making your own? Just cutting back on oil reduces the largest source of calories.

The Perfect All-Purpose Nothing-Artificial Salad Dressing

The best way to dress a homemade salad is, of course, with a homemade dressing.

Here's a 5-minute do-it-yourself dressing:

1 cup low fat yogurt
2 tablespoons wine vinegar
½ small onion, chopped
¼ teaspoon garlic flakes
½ teaspoon dill seeds, crushed
Pinch dry mustard
Freshly ground pepper

• Process all the ingredients in a blender until the onion is completely puréed. Spoon over any combination of leafy greens.

Makes enough dressing for 3 salads. 10 calories per tablespoon.

BALANCING THE WHOLE MEAL SALAD

CROUTONS AND OTHER TOPPINGS

Are you doing the cube? You should be. Those tiny bread cubes called croutons can make a big contribution to the health and heft of your leafy green meals. And if you know enough variations, you can have a different salad on the menu every day.

Make your own croutons by cutting sliced bread into ½-inch cubes. Toss them with a little melted butter, then sauté or bake until golden brown. Can be stored in the refrigerator several days if well covered, but they taste best while they're still hot and toasty.

HOMEMADE CROUTONS

For garlic croutons, rub French bread with peeled garlic halves, brush with olive oil, cut and dice, and broil quickly until crisp and golden. (The croutons will be crisper if you use two-day-old bread instead of fresh bread.)

Did you know that you can even make your own crouton-like creations without bread? Try some of the following:

CORN CHIP TOPPING

2 cups (3–4 ears) cut fresh corn (about 1⅓ cups puréed)
¼ teaspoon onion powder and/or ¼ teaspoon garlic powder (optional)
3 tablespoons chopped green pepper
3 tablespoons chopped unpeeled tomato (including seeds)

• Puree the corn and onion/garlic in a food processor or blender. Spread plastic wrap lengthwise over cookie sheet; tape corners with masking tape. Pour on corn mixture and smooth into a 9 × 13 × ¼-inch rectangle. Sprinkle on the tomato and pepper. Dehydrate 10 hours in a dehydrator or a low oven (150°–200°) until corn can be broken into chip-sized croutons. (Best results can be obtained in dry weather).

Makes 1 cup.

• Separate 4 eggs. Poach the whites in boiling water with a dash of vinegar until firm. Chill and dice. Reserve yolks for another use (see Goldenrod Garnish, next page).

EGG WHITE CROUTONS
(protein without cholesterol and near zero in calories)

GOLDENROD GARNISH
(for non-cholesterol-watchers)

• Place 4 eggs or 4 egg yolks in a small saucepan with cold water to cover. Heat to boiling, lower to simmer and cook 5 minutes until set (or 2 minutes for yolks only). Cool. Press through a sieve to use as a salad garnish. Or dice yolks and scatter over tossed greens.

BAGEL CHIPS

• This works best with mini-bagels which can be bought frozen. Thaw bagel slightly, then slice into paper-thin slices. Sprinkle sparingly with fruit juice. Oven-toast in 325° oven to crunchy sweetness. Only 10 calories per chip.

CHEDDAR CHEESE CROUTONS

¾ cup plus 2 tablespoons flour
¼ teaspoon salt
  Freshly ground pepper, to taste
8 tablespoons butter, softened
1¼ cups grated Cheddar cheese
1 egg, lightly beaten
  Pinch of cayenne

• Preheat oven to 400°.
• Mix the flour, salt and pepper in a bowl and blend in the butter. Add 1 cup of the cheese and knead the mixture until smooth. Turn out onto a lightly floured board and roll out to ¼-inch thickness. Cut into 2-inch squares, then cut each square into 2 triangles. Separate and lay them on a well-greased cookie sheet. Brush lightly with egg.
• Sprinkle with remaining cheese and cayenne, and bake 10–15 minutes until golden. Cool 5 minutes, remove from sheet and serve in salads, chilled or at room temperature.

Makes about 4 dozen.

Variations: Substitute Swiss or Edam for Cheddar; cut into 2-inch squares and serve as a cracker snack to go with salads.

SOFT CHEESE CROUTONS

• Combine 8 ounces of softened Neufchâtel cream cheese with ½ cup chopped sprouts, nuts or finely grated carrot. Form into tiny balls, roll in finely minced parsley and crushed seeds (poppy, caraway, sesame, etc.). Chill and add to salad just before serving, or serve on toothpicks on the side.

SALAD CRACKERJACKS

• Sauté 1 cup cooked corn cut from the cob in a dry skillet until heated through, stirring continuously. Add 1 cup of peanuts and sauté an additional 2 to 3 minutes (if peanuts are dry-roasted, add a little butter). Let stand 30–40 minutes. Season to taste with salt, a substitute or grated cheese. Scatter over salad before serving, or serve on the side in condiment dishes.

Variation: Substitute thawed tiny frozen peas for the corn.

SALAD DOODLES

• Cook 1 package (8 ounces) of ½-inch egg noodles according to package directions. Drain; deep-fry for 2 minutes in 1 inch of 375° oil, turning once. Drain on paper towels. Stir immediately into any hot or room temperature salad.

ROASTER'S CHOICE CROUTONS
(a tasty and low-calorie crouton)

• Bake whole, unpeeled heads of garlic on a rack in a 325° oven for 1 hour. When centers are soft and buttery, cool, pluck off individual cloves and squeeze contents on toasted squares of low-calorie bread. Cut into bite-sized croutons and toss over salads, or serve on the side.

FRUIT SALAD TOPPING

• Toast 1 cup Grape-nuts, plain cornflakes or unseasoned puffed cereal in a 250° oven for 10 minutes. Scatter (warm or cold) over fruit salads.

Variation: Combine with nuts for added crunch.

HOMEMADE RAISINS

• Wash a large bunch of grapes (any variety). Slice each grape lengthwise and remove seeds, if any. Arrange in a single layer on dehydrator trays or cookie sheets and process in a food dryer or in a 150°–200° oven with the oven door ajar until they are shriveled (about 12–24 hours). For best results, dehydrate on a dry day.

Variation: Serve mixed with dry-roasted nuts for added protein and crunch.

FAKE BACON BITS

• Cut squares of tofu into tiny cubes. Soak overnight in liquid hickory-smoke seasoning. Dehydrate under a hot sun or in a low oven or a food dryer until very crisp. Toss or crumble into salads.

NUTTY MIX

4 cups of any raw, shelled, unsalted nuts

• Preheat oven to 250°.
• Spread nuts in a thin layer on a cookie sheet or in baking pans. Dry-roast 30 minutes, stirring at 10-minute intervals. Sprinkle with salt or any substitute (pages 166–168).

CHINESE CHIPS

• The Orient's answer to America's favorite crunchy snack? The low-calorie lotus root. Slice it paper thin, toast it and use it to top salads, or serve on the side. (If your supermarket produce department doesn't carry lotus root, try an Oriental market or see "Mail Order Sources".)

Variation: Use paper-thin slices of ginger root as a spicy substitute.

SHRIMP CHIPS

• A quick fix for potato chip boredom, these uncooked multicolored wafers are available in Chinese markets and markets that sell imported foods, Oriental and otherwise; or order by mail (see "Mail Order Sources"). Simply drop chips in oil heated to 375°; they cook to puffy rainbow-colored crispness in less than 60 seconds.

JAWS
(Crunchy Corn Crackers)

• Preheat oven to 250°.
• In a large bowl combine 3 cups cornmeal and ¼ cup sesame seeds with ½ cup corn oil and 1½ cups boiling water. Add just enough additional water to form a stiff batter. Let cool. Spoon onto a cookie sheet and flatten. Use a pastry or ravioli wheel or a sharp knife to cut into bite-sized crackers (or even tinier croutons). Bake 30 minutes. Cool and break on the scored lines.

Variation: Substitute millet meal in place of cornmeal (a healthier-than-cornmeal whole grain).

FRUIT CRUMBLES

• Peel 4 overripe bananas and slice them as thin as possible. Spread slices on wire racks or cheesecloth-covered trays. Dry under a hot sun outside or in a 150°–200° oven. When dry, crumble and store refrigerated in paper bags.

Variation: Peel and slice ripe apples or pears and dry.

NASTURTIUM BUGLES

8 ounces cream cheese, softened
2 to 3 tablespoons milk
2 teaspoons curry powder
⅛ teaspoon garlic powder
25 dark-colored nasturtium blossoms, washed and
    patted dry (use the leaves or buds of any
    unscented variety)

• Mix together the cheese and milk, blend in curry and garlic powders. Form cheese mixture into tiny balls and spoon one ball into each blossom. Serve in, on, or beside salads, or as a cracker topping or spread.

Variations: Garnish your ready-to-eat salad with ready-to-eat unstuffed blossoms. No nasturtiums? Rosebuds, violets, carnations are all good substitutes.

CORN DIGGERS

1¼ cups yellow cornmeal
½ teaspoon salt or substitute
½ teaspoon baking soda
1 cup plain yogurt
1 tablespoon salad oil
1 teaspoon honey

• Preheat oven to 425°.
• Sift together cornmeal and salt. Stir baking soda into yogurt and blend. Combine mixtures and add remaining ingredients.
• Spread batter thinly on a greased cookie sheet. Bake 10 minutes, then score into triangles, circles or squares. Return to oven and bake 10–15 minutes longer, until crisp.

Variation: Substitute soy grits for cornmeal.

ROASTED ALMONDS

½ pound whole blanched almonds
2 tablespoons unsalted butter
½ teaspoon salt or substitute

• Preheat oven to 350°.
• Spread almonds on a cookie sheet and dot with butter. Season and roast, stirring until lightly browned (8–10 minutes). Immediately remove almonds from cookie sheet and cool on a wire rack.

Variations: Substitute whole cashews or walnuts for the almonds.

Hint: What else is tops instead of croutons? Try 5-Minute Meatballs (page 36), oyster crackers, last night's leftover diced fritters or cold tempura. And when you get tired of toppings, there are always Salad Breads and Crackers (recipes follow).

SALAD SPRINKLES

Use 1 teaspoon or more per serving over hot or cold salads. Use as salt substitutes, seasonings or crouton substitutes. Two types of sprinkles may be combined if desired. Select from these ingredients:

- Unsweetened coconut, toasted.*
- Grated raw carrot, squash or sweet potato.
- Sprouts: alfalfa, soybean, mung bean, chick-pea, wheat, radish, etc.
- Dried vegetable flakes, crushed or powdered.
- Citrus peel, dried and ground or freshly grated (lemon, lime, tangerine, grapefruit or kumquat).
- Toasted seeds: sesame, celery, dill, caraway, poppy, millet, sunflower. etc.
- Granola or Grape-nuts cereal, toasted and crushed.*
- Plain puffed cereal (rice, corn, wheat, toasted).*
- Toasted rolled oats (not instant).*
- Dried mushrooms, toasted and crushed.*
- Shredded wheat biscuits, crushed.
- Wheat germ, corn germ, wheat or oat bran, raw or toasted.
- Cooked corn off the cob.
- Unsalted or dry-roasted nuts (peanuts, almonds, cashews, etc.).
- Finely diced dried fruit.*
- Grated cheese.
- Soy lecithin granules or toasted soy grits.**
- Crushed chips (corn, potato).
- Dry-roasted papaya or pomegranate seeds* (see Papaya Seed Dressing, page 132).

*Best over salads with fruits or sweet vegetables.
**Available at pharmacies, natural food stores, health food sections of supermarkets, or see "Mail Order Sources."

CRACKERS, ETCETERA

If you're crackers for crackers, your best health bet is to roll your own, buy an import or head for the diet food shelves. The typical American cracker has nine times more fat, twice the calories and up to three times more sodium than most imported or special-diet brands. For example, 9 Ritz crackers will add 150 calories, 8 grams of fat and 270 milligrams of sodium to your day's totals.

Read labels before you stock your cracker barrel. My preference for limiting sodium, calories and fat: whole wheat matzos, crisp breads and flat breads, rye or bran wafers, sodium-free or sodium-reduced melba toast, and hardtack (sea biscuits).

Better yet, roll your own.

1–2–3 MELBA TOAST

• Cut slices of leftover bread into vertical strips. Place on a cookie sheet; dry thoroughly for at least 12 hours, uncovered.
• Toast until golden brown in a low oven. Cool on rack.
• Good bread choices: pumpernickel, rye, sprouted wheat, black bread or raisin-nut bread (for fruit salads).

HOMEMADE HARDTACK

• Preheat oven to 450°.
• Mix 1 cup old-fashioned rolled oats, 1½ cups unbleached flour, 1 teaspoon salt or substitute and ½ teaspoon baking soda in a large bowl.
• In a separate bowl, mix ¾ cup buttermilk and 2 tablespoons honey with 2 tablespoons of butter, melted. Combine with the dry ingredients.
• When dough is well mixed, roll out flat to ¼-inch thickness on a lightly greased and floured pizza pan or cookie sheet. Prick dough with a fork and cut into squares, diamonds or triangles.
• Bake for 5 minutes. Timing is crucial (and so is preheating the oven). Finished crackers should be dry, but browned only around the edges.
• Remove from oven, transfer to wire racks to cool and bake any remaining dough without regreasing sheets.
• Store crackers in tightly covered containers to keep crisp.

Makes 6 big crackers or 12 smaller ones.

Variations: Substitute 1 cup of rye meal or 1 cup of cornmeal for 1 cup of oatmeal. Caraway, poppy or sesame seeds may be added for extra crunch.

HERB WHEELS

2 cups rye flour
¾ cup unbleached white flour
½ cup wheat germ or bran
½ teaspoon salt or substitute
1 teaspoon baking powder
6 tablespoons sweet butter, softened, or salad oil
¾ cup milk
1 egg
  Melted butter or fresh lemon juice
1 teaspoon fresh marjoram or savory (or use dried)

• Preheat oven to 325°.
• Combine dry ingredients.
• Cut the softened butter into the dry mixture until it resembles meal. Moisten with the milk beaten with the egg.
• Mix well and roll dough out ¼-inch thick on a lightly floured board. Cut into rounds using a cookie or biscuit cutter.
• Arrange on an ungreased cookie sheet, brush with the butter mixed with the marjoram. Prick biscuits with a fork.
• Bake 20 minutes in a 325° oven or until lightly browned. Cool on racks.

Makes 2 dozen crackers.

CHEESY EGGPLANT STICKS
(only 6 calories per stick, and delicious!)

3 tablespoons puréed tofu
1 tablespoon cold water
2 tablespoons lemon juice
  Garlic powder or garlic juice (optional)
6 tablespoons grated romano or Parmesan cheese
6 tablespoons bread crumbs
1 medium eggplant (1¼ pounds), unpeeled

• Preheat oven to 450°.
• Grease a cookie sheet or shallow baking pan.
• Blend tofu, water, lemon juice and garlic seasoning in a small bowl and set aside. Combine cheese and bread crumbs and spread on wax paper.
• Trim eggplant and cut horizontally into ¾-inch slices, then halve each slice. Dip each stick into the tofu mixture, moistening on both sides. Roll each stick in the cheese mixture to coat. Arrange in a single layer on greased cookie sheet.
• Place cookie sheet on the bottom rack of the oven, bake 5 minutes. Turn eggplant sticks and bake 5 minutes more, until coating is crisp and eggplant is tender.

Makes about 18.

PUMPKINSEED SALAD WAFERS

1½ cups dried pumpkin seeds
2 tablespoons salad oil
1 teaspoon salt or substitute
⅓ cup cornmeal
1½ cups whole wheat flour
⅓ to ½ cup ice water

• Preheat oven to 300°.
• Grind 1 cup of pumpkin seeds in blender. Transfer to a bowl and mix oil and salt with ground seeds.
• Add cornmeal and flour; mix with a fork until mixture is crumbly. Add water, a few drops a time, mixing until dough forms a ball.
• Roll dough on a floured board to ⅛-inch thickness. Score with a sharp knife; prick with a fork. Transfer to an ungreased cookie sheet, sprinkled with remaining ½ cup seeds and bake for 20 minutes, or until lightly browned.

Makes 6 dozen wafers.

Variations: Use 2 cups unbleached white flour in place of cornmeal and whole wheat flour; use cashews, walnuts or pistachios in place of pumpkin seeds.

Hint: Want to make thinny-thin crackers, or wafers you can fill with salad greens or spread with a 30-Second Salad Spread (page 156)? Shape dough in a hand-operated tortilla press (available in housewares departments).

CORIANDER CRACKERS*

2 cups nugget-style unsweetened dry cereal or rolled oats (not the one-minute kind)
¼ cup frozen apple/orange juice concentrate, thawed
1 tablespoon cinnamon
1 teaspoon coriander seeds
¼ cup minced coriander leaves

• Combine all ingredients. Roll out on a greased cookie sheet. Prick all over with an fork, score into 24 squares or 48 triangles. Bake 10 minutes at 350°. Only 10 calories each.

*Coriander seeds have a fragrance reminiscent of aniseed, cumin and orange. Use them whole or ground in cheeses, bean and pasta salads. Coriander seeds even sweeten your breath non-chemically and a crushed seed in the bottom of your teacup makes a welcome change from that habitual lemon peel.

BREADS, WAFERS AND SANDWICHES

PESTO PRESTO SALAD BREAD

Includes the famous sauce's 5 key ingredients: basil, garlic, pine nuts, olive oil and Parmesan cheese.

3 cups unbleached white flour
4 teaspoons baking powder
1 teaspoon salt or 1 teaspoon crushed garlic flakes
⅔ cup grated Parmesan or romano cheese
⅓ cup pine nuts
1 tablespoon minced fresh basil
2 eggs
1½ cups milk
¼ cup olive oil

• Preheat oven to 350°.
• Grease a 9×5×3-inch loaf pan. Combine flour, baking powder, salt or garlic, cheese, pine nuts and basil in mixing bowl. Form a well in the center and add eggs, milk and oil. Mix until moistened (batter will be lumpy). Spoon into pan; bake 50 minutes.
• Cool on a rack. Cut into thin slices.

Makes 1 loaf.

Variations: Substitute melted butter for olive oil; use another nut or seed in place of pine nuts.

HOMEMADE CHINESE BREADSTICKS

3 cups whole wheat flour or unbleached white flour
1 cup wheat germ or bran
1¼ cups whole or skim milk
½ cup salad oil
1 tablespoon honey
1 teaspoon fresh lemon juice
Pinch of Chinese 5-spice powder (optional)
1 cup sesame seeds or as needed

• Preheat oven to 350°.
• Mix together flour, wheat germ, milk, oil, honey, lemon juice and 5-spice powder. Knead dough on a floured board and roll out to ¼-inch thickness. Cut into sticks ¼-inch wide and 5-inches long. Roll lightly in sesame seeds.
• Transfer to a greased baking sheet. Bake 30 minutes or until golden brown. Cool on a wire rack.

Makes 4 dozen sticks.

2 medium cucumbers, peeled
4 tablespoons wheat germ
2 tablespoons cornmeal
3 eggs
1 tablespoon minced parsley

COOL CUCUMBER WAFERS

• Preheat oven to 350°.
• Grate the cucumbers. Mix with the wheat germ and corn-meal. Separate two of the eggs. Beat the yolks with the whole egg and add to the vegetable mixture. Add the parsley and mix well.
• Beat the egg whites until stiff but not dry. Gently fold egg whites into vegetable mixture. Drop by tablespoons on cookie sheet greased with vegetable oil. Bake 20 minutes. Cool on cookie sheet. Carefully cut into squares with a table knife.

Makes 12 wafers.

Variations: Substitute grated carrots, parsnips, summer or winter squash for cucumber or use a grated exotic edible root vegetable.

RYE WAFERS

• Combine 1 cup rye flour with 1 cup unbleached white flour, 1 teaspoon sugar and ½ teaspoon salt. With a fork, stir in ½ cup water and 5 tablespoons salad oil until blended. Turn dough onto a lightly floured board and knead until smooth, about 10 minutes. Shape and bake as for Whole Wheat Wafers, above.

Makes 24 wafers.

VEGETABLE CRISPS

• Prepare any quick biscuit or cracker dough. Sprinkle with dried vegetable flakes or salad herbs. Bake for 3 minutes in a hot waffle iron or flatten in a tortilla press or noodle machine and bake in a microwave oven at "high" for 2 minutes. Break into pieces before serving.

FANCY BUTTER

• Mix into a quarter pound of margarine or butter 2 table-spoons drained, crushed green peppercorns*, 1 large or 2 small cloves garlic, minced, and 1 or 2 dashes of cinnamon.
• Spread on small pieces of plain bread or thin crackers to serve.

WHOLE WHEAT WAFERS

• Preheat oven to 425°.

• Combine 2 cups whole wheat flour and 1½ teaspoons salt or substitute. With a fork, stir in ½ cup plus 2 tablespoons water and 5 tablespoons salad oil until blended. Turn dough onto a lightly floured board and knead until smooth, about 10 minutes. Separate into 16 small rolls of dough. Flatten each in a crisscross fashion with the tines of a fork. Sprinkle with dried onion or green pepper flakes or sesame or poppy seeds and bake until golden, about 10 minutes. Cool on a wire rack.

Makes 16 wafers.

30-SECOND SPREADS

And when tuna/potato/egg salad tedium sets in? Let a salad spread save the day. You can spread these on breads, crackers or chips; stuff celery, cherry tomatoes or peppers; or spread them on leafy greens and roll up for a salad-in-transit snack. You can even scoop them over lettuce leaves and serve as pâté substitutes.

• Mash together a few slices of ripe banana; sprinkle with cayenne, salt or a substitute. Spread and top with sesame seeds.

• Spread a tablespoon of mashed avocado on hot melba toast.

• Mix nut butter and mashed banana with grated carrots or raw sweet potato to offset the dryness. Good scooped over dandelion or collard greens.

• Mix ¼ cup peanut butter, a pinch of dried lemon peel, 1 tablespoon yogurt, 1 small ripe banana. Spread on crisp apple slices. Top with toasted almond flakes.

• Hot for peanuts? Make a fast pâté. Chop 3 cups peanuts in blender; mix in 2 tablespoons prepared horseradish, ⅔ cup plain yogurt and process until thick and smooth.

• Blend chunks of any soft creamy cheese with chopped olives, chopped nuts and fresh spinach leaves. Spread on tortilla chips or diet rice cakes.

• Spread cream cheese mixed with grated orange rind and chopped pecans on thinny-thin slices of fruit-nut bread.

• Purée farmer's cheese with toasted sunflower seeds and alfalfa sprouts. Spread on raw zucchini.

- Purée hard-boiled egg, shredded Cheddar cheese, minced scallions and raw spinach or watercress. Spread on very thin slivers of raw sweet potato.

- Mix together deviled egg, bacon bits, green pepper and shredded lettuce. Scoop over escarole.

- Purée shrimp, scallions and water chestnuts. Spread on raw spinach; sprinkle with herb vinegar.

- Mince together ham and chutney. Spoon into romaine and roll up.

- In a food processor or blender, blend tuna, chopped nuts and spinach leaves. Scoop over shredded Chinese cabbage.

- Purée sardines, hard-boiled eggs and sprouts. Spread on crackers or bread.

- Blend cashew butter, grated carrot and raisins. Scoop over arugula or radicchio leaves.

- Crunchy Salmon Salad Spread: Combine 2 cans drained salmon; 8 ounces cream cheese; 1 tablespoon each prepared horseradish, grated onion and parsley; ¼ teaspoon paprika; ½ cup chopped pecans. Fork-mash until well blended.

- Blend raw spinach, carrots and cauliflower in a food processor. Spread on slices of cucumber, squash, rutabaga or turnip.

- Grind almonds and celery. Moisten with yogurt. Spread on rice wafers or whole wheat pita, or stuff romaine leaves and roll.

- Mash tofu with Calorie-Reduced Mayonnaise (page 134). Add curry and herbs or radish sprouts for crunch and a peppery flavor.

- Fork-mash tofu, blend in chopped celery, grated onion and chopped pickles. Scoop on top of sliced tomatoes, raw turnip or jícama.

- Blend *crème fraîche*, sour cream or yogurt with crushed garlic. Fold in red or black caviar; serve on, or rolled in, lettuce leaves.

- Blend chopped nasturtium or marigold blossoms into cream cheese or mashed tofu. Spread on raw slices of sweet potato or winter squash.

• Combine O.J. Mayo (page 120) with crab, salmon or tuna. Good spread on raw vegetables—or try on cold, cooked beet slices.

• Purée 1 cup tofu with ½ cup ripe avocado and ½ cup shredded iceberg lettuce.

• Soybean Patch Pâté: Chop ¼ cup fresh dill in blender or food processor. Add ¼ cup olive oil and 6 lettuce leaves, 1 tablespoon Worcestershire sauce, 2 tablespoons lemon juice, 1 teaspoon vinegar, 1 minced clove garlic and 1½ cups soft tofu. Blend until creamy.

• Combine 30-second Russian Dressing (page 120) with minced ham. Spread on rice cakes.

• Purée Fast French Dressing (page 119) with lots of grated carrot and cucumber. Serve on raw cucumber slices.

• Purée cooked squash or artichoke hearts with 1 cup fresh watercress or radicchio.

• And for the ultimate use-it-up salad spread? Combine *any* leftover salad with a compatible leftover dressing. Blend in a food processor or blender and spread. To thicken, add lettuce; to thin, add oil.

OLIVE CAVIAR TOASTS

1 small dried chili pepper, seeds removed
1½ cups oil-cured black olives, pitted and diced
1 teaspoon crumbled dried oregano
2 tablespoons olive oil
1 teaspoon lemon juice
3 tablespoons minced onion
  Finely diced hard-boiled eggs
  Melba toast or toasted bread fingers

• Crush pepper with a rolling pin. Combine with olives in a blender or food processor and crush to a coarse paste. Add oregano, oil and lemon juice. Spread on toast and sprinkle with onion flakes and hard-boiled eggs.

12 servings.

Variation: Spread on raw vegetable rounds.

3 croissants, split lengthwise
2 medium-sized carrots, shredded
4 large radishes, shredded
1 cup alfalfa sprouts
2 scallions, sliced
¼ cup sunflower seeds
4 tablespoons any creamy dressing

SUPER SALAD CROISSANTS #1

• Heat croissant halves in preheated 325° oven 10 minutes until crisp; cool slightly. Toss together carrots, radishes, sprouts, scallions and seeds.
• Spoon vegetable mixture over bottoms of croissants. Top each with 1 tablespoon dressing; replace croissant tops and serve.

3 servings.

4 croissants, split lengthwise
4 tablespoons Thousand Island or Russian Dressing (page 128)
1 large avocado, thinly sliced
4 romaine lettuce leaves
1 medium-size red onion, thinly sliced

SUPER SALAD CROISSANTS #2

• Heat split croissants in preheated 325° oven 10 minutes, until crisp; cool slightly.
• Spread bottom half of each croissant with 1 tablespoon dressing; top with avocado, romaine and onion. Replace tops.

4 servings.

3 tablespoons mayonnaise
1 tablespoon lemon juice
2 ounces blue cheese, crumbled
4 cups finely shredded spinach leaves
4 croissants, each slit 1 inch deep along the top

SPINACH AND BLUE CHEESE CROISSANTS

• Preheat oven to 325°.
• Blend mayonnaise and lemon juice in large bowl until smooth. Add blue cheese and spinach; toss until well combined.
• Gently open slit in each croissant and fill with spinach mixture. Place croissants on baking sheets; bake 10 minutes, or until cheese is melted.

4 servings.

FRUIT-FILLED CROISSANTS

8 teaspoons orange marmalade
4 croissants, pockets cut on top
¼ cup chopped pecans

• Preheat oven to 325°.
• Spread 1 teaspoon marmalade in each croissant pocket. Fill with 1 tablespoon pecans then another teaspoon marmalade. Arrange on cookie sheet and bake 10 minutes. Serve hot.

20-CALORIE POTATO SHELLS

2 small baking potatoes, scrubbed and cut in half lengthwise
Parmesan cheese or low-calorie Sapsago grating cheese
Paprika

• Preheat oven to 400°.
• Bake potatoes 30–40 minutes or until soft inside. Scoop out potato, reserving for another use, leaving the shell intact.
• Sprinkle potato skins with cheese and paprika while warm. Broil until brown and crisp. Cut in wedges and serve as a cracker substitute.

Variations: For potato shells slightly higher in calories, fill shells with grated carrot, celery or cucumber before adding cheese and broiling.

HAND-HELD SALADS FOR ONE

Whole-meal salad sandwiches that travel!

• Chèvre, tomato and watercress: Spread 1 ounce French goat cheese on the inside of a small pita pocket; slice in ¼ ripe tomato and a few sprigs of watercress.

• Chicken chutney salad: Combine ½ cup diced cooked chicken; ¼ small apple, diced; 2 tablespoons plain yogurt; 1 teaspoon chutney; ¼ teaspoon curry. Stuff into a small pita pocket and top with alfalfa sprouts.

• Pita taco: Combine ⅛ small avocado, chopped; ¼ small tomato, chopped; and 1 teaspoon each chopped onion, green pepper and chili pepper. Stuff into a small whole wheat pita pocket. Top with 2 tablespoons grated Cheddar cheese and a sprinkling of shredded lettuce.

• Spinach salad: Combine ½ cup shredded spinach with 1 ounce crumbled feta cheese; ¼ small cucumber, chopped; 1 mushroom, sliced; 1 tablespoon chick-peas, and 1½ teaspoons Italian dressing. Toss and stuff mixture into a pita pocket.

• Egg, tomato and basil: Combine 1 chopped hard-boiled egg, 1 tablespoon chopped fresh basil, 1½ tablespoons plain yogurt, 1½ teaspoons mayonnaise, 1 teaspoon minced scallions and salt and pepper to taste; spread on the inside of a small pita pocket. Add ¼ ripe tomato, sliced, and top with 2 tablespoons bean sprouts.

Variation: For even fewer calories, stuff fillings into ultra-low-calorie endive spears instead of pita bread.

THE CONDIMENT SHELF

POTHERB SEASONING

• In seed mill or electric blender, grind mixed dried vegetable flakes with dried mushroom and a small amount of cumin or mustard seeds, plus celery or dill seeds. Experiment with proportions to suit your taste. Spoon into an empty spice jar. Cap tightly and keep dry. Will keep for 3–4 months.

Variation: Add a pinch of kelp or ascorbic acid powder.

SALAD SALT #1

1 tablespoon black peppercorns
1 teaspoon cayenne or crushed red pepper flakes
2 tablespoons garlic flakes or powder
2 tablespoons onion flakes or powder
1 teaspoon soy lecithin granules (optional)
1 tablespoon dried oregano
½ teaspoon mustard seeds or ¼ teaspoon mustard powder (optional)
1 tablespoon salt

• Process as for Potherb Seasoning above. For no-sodium salad seasoning, omit salt.

Makes 6 tablespoons.

SALAD SALT #2

1 tablespoon yeast powder
1 teaspoon thyme
1 teaspoon marjoram
1 teaspoon celery seeds
1 teaspoon garlic flakes or powder
1 teaspoon onion flakes or powder
¼ teaspoon dry mustard
¼ teaspoon cayenne or ½ teaspoon paprika
½ teaspoon lecithin granules (optional)
½ teaspoon ascorbic acid powder or sour salt
½ teaspoon salt

• Follow directions for Potherb Seasoning above. For no-sodium salad seasoning, omit salt.

Makes 5 tablespoons.

SALAD SEASONING

½ cup freshly ground white pepper
¼ cup freshly grated nutmeg
2 tablespoons ground ginger
4 teaspoons ground cloves

• In a small bowl combine all ingredients. Store the mixture in a small jar, tightly covered.

Makes ¾ cup

BELL PEPPER SEASONING

• Add roasted peppers to your salad and you'll never miss the sodium. Place red or green bell peppers on a broiling rack. Broil, turning until all sides are blackened. Skin while warm, seed, and cut into sections. Place in a dish with a dash of white vinegar. Use in any salt-free salad. Store unused peppers in the refrigerator. Will keep for 10 days.

LEMON SEASONING

1 tablespoon dried grated lemon or lime peel
2 tablespoons black peppercorns
1 teaspoon finely grated and dried ginger root (or ½ teaspoon nutmeg)
2 teaspoons powdered kelp or dulse (optional)
1 teaspoon fennel seed

• Grind all ingredients in a mill or crush with a mortar and pestle to a powder. Store in a tightly closed spice jar.

Makes about ¼ cup.

SICHUAN-STYLE SALT

2 teaspoons coarse salt
½ teaspoon Chinese 5-spice powder
¼ teaspoon whole Sichuan peppercorns

• Heat a heavy ungreased skillet over medium heat until hot to the touch. Reduce heat. Add salt, 5-spice powder and peppercorns. Heat, shaking and stirring, until spices give off a pungent odor and the 5-spice powder darkens (6–7 minutes). Strain through a fine-mesh sieve into a small dish; discard peppercorns remaining in sieve. Store in tightly-capped spice jar.

Makes about 2½ teaspoons.

Variation: For a low-sodium alternative, omit the salt.

1 cup blanched whole almonds
2 tablespoons unsalted butter
½ teaspoon celery seed or onion flakes

ALMOND SEASONING

• Heat oven to 350°. Spread almonds on a cookie sheet, dot with butter and season with celery seed or onion flakes. Toast, stirring occasionally, until lightly browned (8–10 minutes).
• Cool, grind in nut mill or blender. Use as a salt substitute, flavor enhancer or salad sprinkle. Store in cool, dry place.

Makes about 1 cup.

4 tablespoons cayenne
3 tablespoons ground cumin
1 teaspoon garlic powder
1 teaspoon ground caraway seeds

MEXICAN SEASONING

• Combine all ingredients; store in a jar with a tight-fitting lid.

GARLIC POWDER

• Commercial garlic powder is made by grinding dehydrated garlic cloves. The fresh cloves are first separated, then the paperlike outer coating is peeled away before dehydration. At home, you can remove the skin from the cloves and slice them to allow air to penetrate more rapidly. Dehydrate in a food dryer or a low oven (150°) overnight; pound to a powder. Powder can be stored and used as you would store-bought, but check strength before substituting.

Variation: For more oomph add a pinch of black or red pepper or dried lemon peel.

¼ cup roasted sesame seeds
1 tablespoon freshly ground pepper
  Pinch lemon peel

SESAME SEASONING

• Combine all ingredients.

Makes about ¼ cup.

Variations: Add 1 tablespoon lightly toasted nutritional or brewer's yeast, or 1 tablespoon store-bought hickory-smoked yeast (sold as a health food seasoning and supplement).

PÂTÉ MAISON SEASONING
(salt-free)

½ tablespoon each: powdered bay leaves, cloves, nutmeg, paprika and thyme
¾ teaspoon each: basil, cinnamon, oregano, sage, savory
¼ cup white peppercorns

• Grind all the ingredients together using a blender or nut/spice grinder. Store in a tightly capped jar. What this traditional French spice mix does for pâté maison, pot roast or stew, it can do for your next roast beef salad. It's even tasty on top of raw vegetable salads.

MUSHROOM SEASONING

• Buy dried mushrooms and grind. The most flavorful mushrooms are Japanese (sweet, light and delicate), and Chilean (mild with a fresh mushroom flavor).

SALT AND NOTHING BUT

• If nothing but salt will do for you, buy a rock-type, kosher style or natural mineral salt that has been minimally processed. These are additive-free and along with the sodium you'll get trace and other minerals generally missing from ordinary salt. Available at gourmet food shops and health food stores.

Keep some of the salt in a salt mill. Grinding your own sodium chloride takes longer than shaking it on but you'll use less because it has more flavor than the packaged stuff.

Herbed Salt

½ cup fresh herbs
½ cup coarse whole salt

• Choose any fresh herb combination that combines well—dill and sweet basil, parsley and rosemary, sage and thyme. Make sure herbs are moisture-free, then whirl in blender with the salt for 2 to 3 minutes. Spread on a cookie sheet, roast in a 120° oven (anything higher will destroy enzymes and flavor) until dry to the touch. When cool, funnel into a shaker jar.

PEPPER

The world's most important spice is indigenous to India and the Far East. It was one of the earliest articles of commerce between the Orient and Europe. In the Middle Ages, rents, dowries and taxes were frequently paid in peppercorns.

Peppercorns are berries that grow on a vine. Green ones are young peppercorns that are pickled in brine or wine vinegar, frozen or air-dried. Black peppercorns are aged on the vine, harvested and then dried. White peppercorns have had their black outside husks removed. The finest quality black peppercorns, darker and more pungent than any others sold, come from Tellicherry on the Malabar coast of India.

Crushed Red Peppers and Powdered Cayenne (Red Pepper). These are botanically related to bell peppers rather than to peppercorns. Both are very hot. Use sparingly.

Sichuan or Chinese Brown Pepper. Aromatic, unusual. Good, spicy alternatives to black pepper.

• Combine ¼ cup each black and white peppercorns and 2 tablespoons whole allspice berries and place in a pepper mill. Use in place of black peppercorns to season any dish.

Makes approximately ½ cup.

Pepper Plus

• Pick and wash young, tender nasturtium seeds. Place in a jar or crock along with one crushed garlic clove; cover with cider vinegar. Tightly cap container and let age at least 30 days. Use in any recipe that calls for capers.

HOMEMADE CAPERS

> 1 pint distilled white vinegar
> ½ cup nasturtium flowers and/or leaves
> 1 clove crushed garlic

"CAPER" VINEGAR

• Wash and dry nasturtium flowers and leaves. Place in a jar with garlic, cover with vinegar and steep at least one month. Vinegar will turn pale yellow. Strain, and pour into a bottle. Add a few fresh blossoms for appearance and cork tightly.
• This makes a good gift for a friend who doesn't garden but appreciates homegrown things.

Makes approximately 2 cups.

ALL-PURPOSE HERB SEASONING

2 cloves garlic
2 teaspoons salt or substitute
½ teaspoon pepper
10 large basil leaves
2 teaspoons sweet marjoram leaves or oregano
4 teaspoons fennel or dill seeds
2 teaspoons poppy seeds

• Put first 6 ingredients in blender and process for 2 minutes. Add poppy seeds and blend until smooth.

Variations: Substitute caraway or celery seeds for poppy seeds.

Hints: Did you know that poppy, dill, caraway and celery seeds taste better freshly ground? You can have them that way in a hurry if you store them in a spare pepper mill and grind just before serving your salad.

HOMEMADE PAPRIKA

• Use 3 ounces of dried chili peppers (mild types such as Anaheim or pasillo, or a combination of mild and hot peppers). Remove and discard stems and seeds. Break up pods and whirl in a blender until finely ground. Let powder settle before removing blender lid.

Makes about ⅓ cup.

Variation: For extra-hot paprika, add to above ⅓ teaspoon each: ground allspice, garlic powder and ground oregano; and ½ teaspoon each ground cloves and coriander. Store in an airtight container. Makes ½ cup.

HOMEMADE MUSTARDS

¼ cup freshly ground mustard seeds (the finer the grind, the smoother the mustard)
5 tablespoons dry mustard
½ cup hot water
¾ cup distilled white vinegar
2 tablespoons cold water
2 large slices onion (approximately 1 ounce)
2 teaspoons honey
1 teaspoon unsulfured molasses
2 cloves garlic, peeled and halved
¼ teaspoon dill seeds
¼ teaspoon ground cinnamon
¼ teaspoon ground allspice
¼ teaspoon dried tarragon, crumbled
¼ teaspoon ground cloves

BASIC GRAIN MUSTARD

• Soak the ground mustard seed and dry mustard in ½ cup hot water with ¼ cup of the vinegar at room temperature for 3 hours.

• Combine cinnamon, allspice, tarragon and cloves in a small saucepan with remaining vinegar, 2 tablespoons cold water, the honey, molasses, garlic, dill seeds and onion. Bring to a boil and boil 1 minute. Remove from heat, cover, and let stand 1 hour.

• Transfer mustard mixture to the blender. Strain the liquid from the spice mix into the mustard mixture, pressing the spices against the sides of the strainer to extract the flavor. Process the mustard mixture until it's a puree-like consistency.

• Put mixture into the top of a double boiler over simmering water and cook until thick (20–25 minutes). Mustard will thicken as it cools.

• Remove from heat and pour into a jar. Cool, cap and refrigerate.

Makes about 2½ cups.

BASIC SALAD MUSTARD

½ cup dry mustard
½ cup hot water
6 tablespoons distilled white vinegar
¼ teaspoon garlic powder
  Pinch of dried tarragon
½ teaspoon unsulfured molasses or honey

• Soak the mustard in the hot water with 1 tablespoon of vinegar. Let it set for 2 hours.

• Combine the remaining vinegar with the garlic and tarragon in a separate bowl and let stand 30 minutes; then strain and add the liquid to the mustard mixture.

• Add molasses or honey. Pour mustard into the top of a double boiler over simmering water. Cook until thick, about 15 minutes (mustard will thicken further when chilled). Remove from heat. Cool and spoon into a jar. Refrigerate. Bonus: This mustard is low in sodium because it's salt-free.

Makes 1 cup.

HOMEMADE FLAVORED VINEGARS

Flavored vinegars are a cinch to make, and worth it, because a good vinegar is all you need to toss a fast and tasty salad. And unlike oil, it's near-zero in calories and sodium-free.*

All you need is colored glass wine bottles or glass jars, corks, a small funnel, cheesecloth or a strainer, a plain vinegar or your choice (white vinegar displays an herb's color; apple cider vinegar is more nutritious; natural wine vinegars taste best), and herbs, seeds, fruit or vegetables.

BASIC HERB OR SEED VINEGAR WITH GARLIC

5 sprigs fresh herbs (rosemary, sage) or 1 tablespoon caraway, celery or other seed
3 to 4 cloves garlic, peeled
1 quart white wine vinegar or cider vinegar

• Heat vinegar to a boil in an noncorrosive enamel or stainless steel pot.
• Place herbs or seeds and garlic in a clean, heat-proof jar or bottle.
• Pour in hot vinegar. Let cool uncovered. Cap tightly.
• Let flavors marry at least a week. Strain and decant into a glass jar or wine bottle. (For a stronger flavor, crush some of the garlic or seeds before steeping.)

HERB VINEGAR

1 cup red wine vinegar
¼ cup fresh dill or ½ teaspoon dried dill
¼ cup snipped fresh chives or 1 tablespoon dried chives
½ cup snipped fresh mint or 2 tablespoons dried mint
1 clove garlic, finely chopped

• Combine all ingredients and refrigerate in a covered container overnight or longer to allow flavor to develop. Strain before using to remove herbs.

Makes 1 cup.

---

*If you're really serious, you can make your own vinegar. You should start with good wine and use a *mère de vinaigre* (mother of vinegar), the basis of a fungus that converts the wine into vinegar. The best way to get both is to order a vinegar kit which comes with half a gallon of wine, mother, recipes and instructions, a carafe, a stand for the barrel and a funnel. Ask your wine dealer for the nearest source. Or see "Mail Order Sources."

BASIC FRESH FRUIT VINEGAR

1 quart fresh fruit (raspberries, blueberries, strawberries, etc.)
1 quart distilled white or cider vinegar

• Crush or chop the fruit coarsely.
• Heat vinegar in noncorrosive pot. Turn off heat, add fruit, and continue as for Basic Vinegar above.

FLOWER VINEGAR

• Fill a pint jar loosely with flowers and leaves (washed and shaken dry) of any edible flower.* Fill to the top with a preheated and cooled mild apple cider or rice vinegar. Cover tightly and set in a dark place to age for two weeks. Strain into a wine bottle or decanter.

SHORTCUT VINEGARS

Pour half the contents of a 1-quart bottle of wine vinegar or cider vinegar into a pitcher or measuring cup and set aside. Place choice of vinegar seasonings below in vinegar bottle, then pour reserved vinegar back in and cap. Let sit in a sunny window for 2–4 weeks for the flavor to develop. Then filter the vinegar, cap tightly and store until ready to use. Here are some combinations to try:

To cider/white wine vinegar add any of the following:

- • 1–2 tablespoons crushed raspberries and 1 teaspoon honey.

- • A few sprigs of fresh dill, thyme or tarragon.

- • Lemon juice and twists of lemon or lime rind.

- • A splash of sherry and a cinnamon stick.

To red wine vinegar add any of these:

- • A dash of anisette, a garlic clove and a few whole capers. (Remove the garlic from vinegar after 24 hours.)

- • A slice of fresh ginger.

- • A few parsley sprigs and black peppercorns.

*See "Edible Flowers" (page 33).

HINTS AND TIPS

FEEDING YOUR SALAD: CALORIES AND NUTRIENTS

A salad is the ideal diet and health food, or is it? That all depends on what you toss. (Iceberg lettuce, for example, has more calories than romaine, only 10% as much vitamin A as endive, and less vitamin C than spinach.) And what you toss it *with*. (Regular blue cheese dressing is 25 times more fattening than lowfat blue, but has more vitamins A and D.) And what you toss on top. (Grated cheese has twice the calories of grated carrot but twice the calcium, too.)

Not to mention what you munch on the side. Pickles add crunch, potato chips add calories and hard-boiled eggs offer low-calorie protein. But the list doesn't stop there. Anything goes in salads these days, so it helps to know what else you're tossing calorically and nutritionally in your at-home or away-from-home salad bar.

GREENS*	CALORIES	NUTRIENTS
Head lettuces (including iceberg, crisphead)	10 calories a cup	The least nutritious salad green; moderate in calcium, potassium, some vitamin C, low in sodium
Loose-leaf lettuces (including oak-tip, ruby)	8 calories a cup	High in calcium, potassium and C; a top source of vitamin A; low in sodium
Butterhead lettuces (buttercrunch, Boston)	8 calories a cup	Half the vitamin A of loose-leaf; twice the iron and triple the vitamin C
New Zealand spinach/ spinach	5–6 calories a cup	High in vitamins A and C, calcium, potassiuum
Kale	6–8 calories a cup	Tops for vitamin C and calciuum; 300% more vitamin A than head lettuce
Collards	6–8 calories a cup	Best dark green for protein/calcium; 300% more vitamin C than iceberg
Beet greens	6–8 calories a cup	Twice the iron of most greens
Sorrel	6–8 calories a cup	Super source of vitamins A and C, potassium; twice the calcium of iceberg
Swiss chard	6–8 calories a cup	Tops in calcium, vitamin A and iron; second best green source of potassium after parsley
Arugula	6–8 calories a cup	Four times more calcium than most greens; as much iron as chard
Endive	6–8 calories a cup	Half as nutritious as beet greens; twice as vitamin-rich as iceberg

*All greens are a good source of fiber and iron.

DRESSINGS AND OILS	CALORIES	NUTRIENTS
Oil and vinegar	94 per Tbs.	Protein; minimal amounts A, D, E
Blue or Roquefort	80 per Tbs.	Protein; minimal amounts A, D, E
French, Italian, Russian	60 per Tbs.	Protein; minimal amounts A, D, E
Lowfat blue cheese	3 per Tbs.	Protein; minimal amounts A, D, E
Lowfat thousand island	27 per Tbs.	Protein; minimal amounts A, D, E
Lowfat Italian	8 per Tbs.	Protein; minimal amounts A, D, E
Lowfat French	5 per Tbs.	Protein; minimal amounts A, D, E
Guacamole/sour cream	30 per Tbs.	Protein; minimal amounts A, D, E
Salad oil	125 per Tbs.	Protein; minimal amounts A, D, E
Mayonnaise	100 per Tbs.	Protein; minimal amounts A, D, E

CHEESE	CALORIES	NUTRIENTS
Cheddar	113 per oz.	Protein, calcium, vitamin B
Mozzarella, whole and part skim-milk	80 per oz.	Protein, calcium, vitamin B
Cream cheese	100 per oz.	Protein, calcium, vitamin B
Cottage cheese, creamed	30 per oz.	Protein, calcium, vitamin B
Swiss	110 per oz.	Protein, calcium, vitamin B
Feta	75 per oz.	Protein, calcium, vitamin B
Yogurt, plain	130 per cup	Calcium, B, phosphorus

MISCELLANEOUS	CALORIES	NUTRIENTS
Raw vegetables (radishes, green peppers, mushrooms, etc.)	about 10 per oz.	Vitamins A, B, C; fiber, calcium, iron
Croutons	50 per ½ cup	Fiber; B vitamins
Bacon bits	30 per Tbs.	Minimal
Sprouts	10 per oz.	Vitamins A, C; minerals, protein
Banana flakes	170 per ½ cup	Potassium
Cooked soybeans	120 per ½ cup	B vitamins; protein
Chick-peas (garbanzos)	140 per ½ cup	Vitamins A, B; protein
Pistachios	90 per 30 nuts	Protein; B vitamins
Cashews	350 per 30 nuts	B vitamins; calcium
Almonds, roasted	178 per oz.	B vitamins; calcium
Tortilla chips	150 per oz.	B vitamins; calcium
Canned fried onion rings	170 per oz.	Minimal
Olives, green	50 per 10	Minimal
Olives, black	60 per 10	Minimal
Olives, salt-cured	90 per 10	Minimal
Caviar	42 per Tbs.	Iron, protein
Pickle relish	14 per Tbs.	Minimal
Pickles, sour	50 per oz.	Minimal
Cooked pasta	120 per cup	Carbohydrates; B vitamins

MISCELLANEOUS (cont'd.)	CALORIES	NUTRIENTS
Potato chips	160 per oz.	Minimal
Corn chips	160 per oz.	Minimal
Potato sticks	150 per oz.	Minimal
Pretzels	60–120 per oz.	Minimal
10 cheese straws	272 calories	Minimal
Sunflower seeds	170 per oz.	Vitamins A, B; protein
Pumpkin seeds	144 per 3 Tbs.	Phosphorus, iron; vitamin C
Caraway, poppy seeds	60 per Tbs.	B vitamins
Peanuts, crushed	55 per Tbs.	Protein; B vitamins
"Light" peanuts, crushed	35 per Tbs.	Protein, plus reduced fat and calories
Pecans	200 per ¼ cup.	B vitamins; protein

Toss-Ins

Give your favorite salad add-in the texture test for nutritional value. A vegetable's texture is a key to the vitamin it contains:
• If it's *juicy* (tomatoes, melon), you're getting vitamins A and C.
• If it's *chewy* (sprouts), you're getting vitamins B and D.
• If it's *crunchy* (nuts, all greens, raw vegetables), you're getting vitamins A, B and C.
• *Oily* means vitamin E.
• *Mushy* (avocados, mangos) means A and B.
• And the *darker in color* a green is (kale, spinach, beet tops) the more vitamins and minerals it probably supplies.

What's In an Herb

Add an herb, sprout or even flower for extra nutrition without many calories.
• *Vitamin A*: alfalfa, dandelion, oregano, sage, red pepper and paprika, basil, sorrel, parsley, rosebuds, violets.
• *Vitamin C*: paprika, oregano, parsley, rose hips, watercress, nasturtium leaves or blossoms, basil, violets, rose leaves or buds, amaranth leaves, seeds or sprouts.
• *Vitamin D*: watercress.
• *Vitamin B*: oregano, paprika.
• *Vitamin E*: alfalfa, dandelion leaves or buds, watercress, celery leaves or seeds.
• *Calcium*: chives, basil, dandelion, nettle, sorrel, nasturtium leaves or flowers, arrowroot, amaranth, chamomile.

• *Iron*: mullein, nettle, parsley, tarragon, nasturtium, amaranth, burdock.
• *Magnesium*: carrot tops, dandelion, meadowsweet, mullein, parsley, peppermint, watercress.
• *Potassium*: carrot tops, chamomile, comfrey, dandelion, fennel, mullein, nettle, parsley, peppermint, primrose flowers, savory, watercress, yarrow.
• *Protein*: alfalfa, amaranth, comfrey, any sprouted seed.
• *Protein; minerals; vitamins A, B and C*: all sprouts.

Six Salad Bar Survival Tips

How fattening is that "chef's special" at your favorite restaurant? Here's the countdown for a few whole meal favorites eaten out:

1. Spinach and mushroom salad: High in fiber, an unbeatable low-calorie choice, but to make up for the missing thiamine, calcium and protein, ask for a few slices of turkey or chicken on the side, or cheese and crackers.

2. A cold shrimp salad in an avocado? A good, moderate-calorie choice (400 for ¾ cup of salad with avocado, hold the mayo).

3. Classic tuna salad plate (tomato and cucumber slices, lettuce, hard-boiled egg wedges plus ¾ cup tuna salad): Delivers calcium magnesium and thiamine. Try adding yogurt, grapefruit and sunflower seeds to boost missing nutrients.

4. Skimp on the chips, not the greens, which add vitamins A, C and fiber.

5. Better to leave out dressing and switch to lemon juice or vinegar with herbs.

6. To add protein to diet salads, crabmeat beats cold cuts. Beef has 5 times the calories of seafood, more fat and less protein.

7. Most salad dressings are high in fat. You get half a cup of fatty dressing if it's not served on the side. But three tablespoons is all you need, so do it yourself. And to cut down on fat at home, change the oil and vinegar proportions to 4 to 1 (not 3 to 1) to reduce fat. Compensate with extra herbs, garlic and mustard.

What's better than a month of sundaes? A month of salads. Let your fingers do the tossing to lose weight and feel great.

With the last mouthful comes the first regret, as the saying goes. A no-regrets way to diet? Eat six meals a day instead of three. Just divide your usual portions in half. When the going gets tough, try mentally eating the food you crave. Close your eyes and imagine what it would be like to enjoy a doughnut. "Eating" food mentally often satisfies cravings.

Today, fill up with Lettuce-Free Salad (pages 48, 49) and have Cheesy Eggplant Sticks (page 152) on the side. Only *190* calories for the combination.

Don't try any diet more than once. Even if you lost some weight the first time, physical activity, metabolism, body chemistry and life style may have changed between the time you first tried the diet and the second time around. Also, repeaters tend to be cheaters. And if it didn't work before, going back to a diet reminds you that you failed the first time. Most dieters do better with a program that has no association of failure attached.

If you want a salad you can come back to for seconds, make a Wheat Berry Salad (page 63). Only *200* calories a carbohydrate-filled bowlful.

Drink an 8-ounce glass of water whenever you get the urge to snack. Lots of water dampens the appetite and helps flush out the excess sodium that causes a bloated look.

Today, try a New Potato Salad (page 115). Only *150* calories for a small but satisfying serving.

Counting on "health food" to slim you down? Count right. The five most caloric choices at salad bars (95 calories per ½ cup or more) include: bean salad, cranberry sauce, potato salad, sunflower seeds, tahini (sesame paste) dip. Even plain mayonnaise will set you back about 100 calories a tablespoon. The five least fattening items (besides those parsley sprigs): carrot strips, lettuce, mushrooms, radishes and sprouts are your best bets.

Today, have a Vegetable Vegetarian Salad (page 57). Only *160* calories a serving.

30-Day Salad-a-Day Diet

Day One

Day Two

Day Three

Day Four

Day Five

Appetite up? Energy down? It's probably three o'clock. This is the time of day most of us reach for sweets, but be smart and reach for celery and carrot sticks instead.

Today have Ham and Cheese Coleslaw (page 114). Only *125* calories a cup.

Day Six

Saving your calories for a high-calorie Italian dessert? Here's what you get from four favorites: biscuit tortoni (½ cup), 431 calories; cannoli (1), 194 calories; Neopolitan torte (¹⁄₁₂ of 10″ cake), 560 calories; and spumoni (½ cup), 464 calories.

Today, have a 175-calorie-a-helping Au Jus Beef Salad (page 104) with plain popcorn on the side.

Day Seven

Are you aerobic phobic? Although everyone should get some exercise, you won't have to exercise more to weigh less if you cut back on a few of your favorite breakfast foods. Substitute unbuttered toast for a Danish 5 times a week for a weight loss of about 6 pounds a year. Eliminate 3 teaspoons of sugar a day in your coffee for a loss of about 4½ pounds a year. Or eat only 1 egg 3 times a week instead of 2 eggs 3 times a week to lose about 3½ pounds a year.

Today, have a Double Radish Salad (page 59). *100* calories a tossing.

Day Eight

Boob tube turning you into blob? Don't munch; sip something that lasts clear through the Late Late Show and adds less than 100 calories to a day's total.

Today, a Vegetarian Antipasto Salad (page 66). Ups your eater's ante only *155* calories.

Day Nine

Turning off the lights before you eat turns the appetite down. Studies show that fewer calories are consumed because you tend to eat less when you can't see what you're eating.

A clear winner to eat when the lights are down low—Cactus Crabmeat Salad (page 90). Only *160* calories a cup. And to cut the calories of the cheese ingredient by 50 percent, use cubes of part-skim Edam on top.

Day Ten

If you can't stand the calories, stay out of the kitchen. If you're tipping the scales, you're secreting extra insulin when you see or smell food. Extra insulin (a hormone produced in the pancreas) leads to an extra large appetite and promotes the storage of fat in the body.

Today, have a fat-fighting Arugula/Endive Salad (page 69). Only *165* calories a toss.

Four great vegetable juices for controlling a runaway appetite? Carrot, celery, spinach and beet.

And if you love beets a lot, have a healthy Fruit and Fiber Salad (page 39) today. Only *180* calories a platter.

It takes 5½ large heads of iceberg lettuce to do the caloric damage of just 1 cup of 400-calorie-a-cup chili with beans.

Pass up that diet-buster and have a Simple Soybean Salad (page 51) instead. *200* calories a bowl.

Five new juicy-fruit fruit salad fruits with better-than-banana calorie counts? Try fresh cherimoya, ugli fruit, mango, papaya or passion fruit.

Or today, make a B.L.T. Plus (page 112). Only *150* calories a cup.

Washing down your coleslaw with wine? Watch it! Nothing's quicker than liquor for putting on pounds. Biggest offenders? Muscatel and port, with twice the calories-per-drink (160) of dry sherry or champagne (85). A few more numbers to note: sweet vermouth (200), egg nog (335), mint julep (212), Tom Collins and old-fashioned (280). Lowest calories of all? Dry wine (85), light beer (95–150), sparkling mineral water and seltzer (0).

Today, with a small glass of dry wine, have a small Mussel, Shrimp and Scallop Salad (page 86). Only *220* calories a serving.

When you feel like you could eat your head off, grab hunger by the ears. An acupressure technique to put the brake on nibbling: Insert index fingers gently into your ears with palms turned toward face. Place thumbs on the little bump of cartilage at the front of the ear. Massage this bump between thumbs and index fingers for a minute or more. An alternative technique: Find the small depression in front of your ears; rub with index fingers, using a circular motion, for a minute or two.

Today, fight hunger and build health with a Spring Greens Chicken Salad (page 99) or a Mixed Rocket Pocket Salad (page 62). Only *150* calories each.

Day Sixteen

To eat out and keep calories low, eat ethnic. Typical meal totals? Mexican, 512; Italian, 941; and Chinese, 1,247. Two unusually high in sodium as well as calories are American and Middle Eastern. (Excess salt causes water retention and temporary weight hikes).

Today, eat ethnic at home. Have a Jícama-Orange Salad (page 54). Only *175* calories a serving.

Day Seventeen

Tipping the scales after a special occasion or holiday celebration? Repent for a few days with baby foods seasoned with no-cal spices/herbs to improve flavor. Those 3-ounce jars of baby foods aren't half bad as a whole meal with salad on the side. Try puréed apricot for a fruit-mousse substitute or spinach and eggs baked as a crust-free quiche. And it's easy to control calories because each jar averages 100 calories.

Today, have a big bowl of small-on-calories Hearts of the East Salad (page 45). Only *150* calories a cup.

Day Eighteen

Baby your appetite. Smaller plates and mini utensils trick you into taking smaller portions and eating few calories. Variety stores carry knife and fork sets for toddlers. Or if you live on yogurt, invest in a set of demitasse spoons. If you're a traveling dieter, buy one set for home and one for the road.

Today, put Self-Dressing Salad #1 (page 64) on your menu. Only *130* calories a serving.

Day Nineteen

Scientists say that the average kiss burns six to twelve calories. At the rate of two kisses a day—one in the morning and one at night—in one year you could lose 2½ pounds. Besides a lot of love, have a lot of salad.

Today, try Cabbage Patch Slaw (page 93). Only *150* calories a cup.

Day Twenty

So-called health foods can have pretty hefty calorie counts. Watch these salad extras: banana chips, 40 calories per ounce; dry-roasted almonds, 170 calories an ounce; sesame tahini, 70 calories per tablespoon; unbuttered pita (pocket) bread, 160 calories each; chick-peas, 100 calories a cup; and pistachios, 150 calories a handful.

Today try a bowl of *175*-calorie-a-helping Salmon-Stuffed Endive (page 88).

Day Twenty-One

Can't reverse your eating impulses? Eat a little more and walk it off. Did you know that rapid walking burns 350 calories an hour—enough to cause a weight loss of ¾ pound a week?

Today, improve your mood with a recap of Au Jus Beef Salad (page 104). Only *250* calories a serving.

Day Twenty-Two

More can be less. To cut down on calories, trick your eyes into thinking you're eating a lot with bulky low-calorie foods that give the illusion you're eating more: Lettuce and cabbage take up a lot of space but have few calories. Ditto high-water fruits and vegetables, such as melon and tomatoes. And unbuttered popcorn instead of potato chips serves the same purpose.

Today, have a big high-fiber low-calorie Chèvre Salad with Cucumber and Purple Basil (page 44). Only *200* calories a serving.

Day Twenty-Three

What's your fat-facts IQ? Did you know that filet mignon has half the calories of prime rib; or that 3½ ounces of water-packed tuna is 160 calories lower than the same amount of oil-packed with 20 percent more protein; or that 30 pistachios have 90 calories while 30 cashews have 350 calories?

Today, you can have a Half-a-Minute Salad (pages 117, 118) with any 30-Second Dressing (pages 119, 120) and have seconds. Less than *300* calories for the combination.

Day Twenty-Four

Are cheese-and-cracker snacks doing your diet in? Switch from saltines to raw zucchini slices and spread with 10-calorie-a-tablespoon Mock Boursin: Mix ½ cup of uncreamed cottage, pot or farmer's cheese with 1 mashed clove of garlic. Add plenty of chopped parsley, freshly ground pepper and Italian herbs; blend and chill. A good peanut substitute on the side? Raw green peas fresh from the pod.

Today, have any mixed green salad with Red, White and Blue Pepper and Cheese Salad Dressing (page 138) on top. Only *215* calories a serving.

Day Twenty-Five

Do you brake for salad bars? If you do, pass up the high-calorie crackers (7 Triscuits have as many calories as a scoop of chocolate ice cream), for plain Melba toast instead.

Today, help yourself to Ham and Cheese Coleslaw (page 114). Only *175* calories a serving.

Day Twenty-Six

Substitutes can save your dieting day. Stock your pantry with snacks you don't have to sneak. Six with less than 100 calories: a small baked potato; one sliver of angel food cake; 28 chocolate chips; 20 fresh slices of mango or kiwi; 1 cup of popcorn sprinkled with Parmesan cheese; one mug of chicken bouillon. And if you love guacamole, use asparagus in place of avocados (23 calories vs. 145).

Today, have a Nature's Bowl #1 (pages 60, 61) with a few thin Bagel Chips (page 146) or one fat pickle. Only *190* calories a bowl.

Day Twenty-Seven

Become a busy body. A more athletic body makes more efficient use of food, say exercise physiologists.

Today, serve yourself a 30-Second Salad Spread (page 156) on low-calorie crackers with sprouts on the side.

Day Twenty-Eight

Do you want to pig out? Then work out! It's possible to increase your metabolism by 46 percent if you exercise regularly. Thirty minutes of vigorous daily exercise improves the ability of muscle cells to burn more fat even while you sleep.

Today, put Thick and Creamy Mustard Dressing (page 136) on your nearly-no-calorie spinach greens. Only *100* calories a dressed-up serving.

Day Twenty-Nine

Try a little obedience training for your appetite. Freeze herb tea or diet soda in ice cube trays. When you get the urge to nibble, suck on a cube. It keeps your mouth filled and your hunger fulfilled.

Today, have a Canadian Bacon Salad with Curry Dressing (page 111). Only *175* calories for a super serving.

Day Thirty

"No matter what kind of diet you're on, you can usually eat as much as you want of anything you don't like," someone once observed. Salads, fortunately, are the exception.

Today, have a Fusilli Salad with Creamy Basil Dressing (page 67) and have your fill. Only *150* calories a serving.

EQUIPMENT

What's the minimal daily requirement for a well-equipped salad kitchen? Here are some tools that you shouldn't be without.

Chopping Board: A heavy board of unfinished wood is best. See if you can find one that comes with a half-cup measuring gadget in the corner so you can chop, dice and measure foods all at once.

Chopping Bowl with Metal Chopper Attachment: For chopping eggs, onions, root vegetables, even meats.

Colander: This large footed strainer for washing and draining vegetables and greens will double as a crisper.

Cruets: You need a pair to hold the oil and vinegar or dressing salads at the table. An old-fashioned caster to hold them along with other condiments, while not necessary, is nice.

Electric Blender/Food Processor: Invaluable for blending dressing ingredients, making salad spreads, grinding seeds and nuts, and much more.

Food Mill or Ricer: For mashing and grating foods *without* puréeing them.

French Salad Basket: A folding mesh basket that is easily stored is indispensable for draining and crisping greens.

Garlic Press: Use this not just to crush garlic cloves, but to extract juice from ginger root, and to extract juice from lemon or lime slices.

Graters: A drumlike revolving grater with a hopper and handle will simplify cheese grating and nut crushing.

Nutmeg Grater or Mill: For grating whole nutmeg and cinnamon sticks.

Pepper Mill/Salt Grinder: For grinding coarse salt and peppercorns. Also for grinding whole spices.

Potato Peeler and a Handheld Slicer: For shredding and paring raw vegetables and fruits.

Glass Jars and Bottles: For mixing and storing home-made dressings and seasonings.

Salad Bowls: The bigger the better. Two can be served

from a big bowl, but you can't serve six or eight from a small one.

Six Individual Salad Bowls plus Chef-Size Salad Bowl: For complete meal salad servings. The ultimate bowl is one carved from a single piece of olive wood. Good wooden bowls of any type should be of unfinished wood, never varnished (wood must be porous to absorb some of the oils and dressing). Preseason your wooden bowl by rubbing lightly with oil. Before and after each use, clean carefully. Many salad pros insist that salad bowls should never be washed, just wiped well with paper towels or a damp cloth after using. And *never* soak a wooden bowl in water or put it in the dishwasher.

The following items may make your salad-making days more enjoyable.

Salad Dryers: Taking your greens for a spin? You don't need a spinner or a dryer, but you'll never regret it if you buy one. The salad dryer dries greens more efficiently than towels and reduces the process to seconds rather than minutes. It can be used in the sink, saving counter space, and it dries greens better so they stay crisper and keep longer. Prices range from $10 to $20 for a manual model, twice that if it's electric.

A Fluting Knife: Does a good job of fluting root vegetables like turnips, making crinkle-cut raw carrots, and so on.

A Tomato Cutter/Hard-Boiled Egg Slicer: One with V-shaped stainless steel teeth will turn tomatoes, radishes, beets, eggs and more into star-shaped salad garnishes.

Mayonnaise Whipper and Dispenser: Makes half a pint of mayonnaise in a minute.

Butter-Decorators: Wooden paddles make crisscross-surfaced butter balls and a fluted curler forms a thin shell of butter when drawn along the surface.

TIPS FOR TOSSERS

• When's a radish not a radish? When it's a rose. To make one, trim off the root end from a red radish and, with a sharp knife, make petal-shaped leaves by cutting down the sides around the radish from the top, close to the skin. Chill in ice water until petals open.

• To make carrot curls, remove strips by pulling a vegetable peeler lengthwise along the surface of the carrot. If the strips don't curl, coil each around your finger, fasten with a toothpick and refrigerate in ice water to crisp.

• To make celery fans, cut inner stalks of celery into 1½-inch lengths; make thin slits at one or both ends and put in ice water to crisp.

• To flute a cucumber, draw a fork lengthwise from one end to the other, scoring the entire surface. Slice crosswise into thin slices and crisp in ice water.

• Swiss cheese should be sliced super thin and served at room temperature to taste its nutty best in salads.

• If you have to make tomorrow's salad today: Fix a salad two hours, even two days, in advance. Clean the salad vegetables, cut into bite-sized pieces. In a nonporous bowl (wood absorbs oils) pour in one or two tablespoons per serving of dressing. Place the sturdier greens on top of dressing, top with smaller, more delicate leaves. Add or arrange other vegetables, garnishes or fruit. Cover tightly with clear plastic wrap and refrigerate. As long as greens don't mix with the dressing, they don't wilt. In fact, salads prepared in advance often taste better.

• To revive limp carrots, celery or greens, soak 60 minutes in ice water. Add a teaspoon of honey to seal in flavor.

• Tossing a salad with dressing that has been placed in the *bottom* of the bowl instead of poured over the top coats greens better with less dressing.

• To improve the eye appeal of a large serving bowl of salad, arrange colorful borders on top of greens around the edge of the bowl. Alternate slices of beets, meats, cucumber or avocado, or pepper rings. Use tomato wedges or cherry tomatoes to circle the top of the salad. If you use cherry tomatoes, cut them in half so they can be easily speared.

• Before peeling oranges or grapefruit for salads, heat them for a few minutes in a hot oven, or 60 seconds in the microwave. The white stringy inner fibers will come off easily when the heated skin is removed.

• Put the dressing for a fresh fruit salad into the bowl first, then drop each piece of fruit into the bowl as it's cut. By quickly dressing the fruit, it won't darken.

• To keep snow white mushrooms snow white, refrigerate in a brown paper bag instead of a plastic one. And to prepare them quickly, use an egg slicer for neat, even slices.

• Do your tomatoes need a lift? A pinch of sugar improves their flavor.

• Doubling a salad recipe? Don't double the salt or the salt substitute. Only increase by half the amount, being sure to taste before you shake. Every shake of the salt cellar adds 100 milligrams of sodium.

• Four better-than-pepper salad pepper-uppers? Watercress, geranium leaves (any variety with unscented leaves), sprouted radish or sunflower seeds, basil. And if you grow your own carnations, make that five (the cinnamonlike buds are edible).

• Six best herbs for salad-making if your pantry's petite: basil, thyme, oregano, parsley, dill and tarragon.

• Brightly colored grated carrots, beets or shredded red cabbage liven up any salad.

• Is there any shelf life left in your spices and herbs? You'll know if you write the date on small pieces of tape and stick to the bottom of each jar when purchased. Most spices and herbs should be replaced six months after purchase date.

• A sprinkle of grated lemon peel over salads makes them taste fresher.

• For long-life mushrooms: String fresh ones on a thread and hang in a warm, dry attic for two weeks, or freeze them after blanching in water for one minute. Store on a dry pantry shelf. If you used the first method, save half a cup to grind into an instant salt substitute. All you add is a pinch of pepper.

• How to ripen a rock-hard avocado for guacamole? Give it a two-minute roast in a microwave set at medium.

• For "Emergency Green Goddess Dressing," peel and purée an avocado, add lemon juice and pepper and freeze in ice cube trays. Defrost a cube for a salad dressing starter.

• Turn a leaf and lift your mood. All green vegetables (and especially spinach) are rich in folic acid, a B vitamin that is said to improve memory and mood and help fight infections.

• What salad-bowl flower supplies more calcium than lettuce? Nasturtium. Use the leaves or buds of any unscented variety.

• Put a little protein in your salad bowl without adding fish or fowl. Corn (5 gm.); spinach (6 gm.); potato (3 gm.); rice (4 gm.) per one cup serving.

• Need onion juice in a hurry? Cut a slice from the top of an onion and sprinkle with salt. Let sit for 10 minutes, then scrape onion surface with a sharp knife.

• Out of soy sauce? Substitute 3 parts Worcestershire mixed with 1 part water.

• Lemon-less? Use vinegar—but only half as much.

• Yes. Oil and vinegar *always* mix, if you add 1 teaspoonful of soy lecithin to each cup of oil, and shake well before you add the vinegar and herbs.

• Did you know that to prevent the awkward mess of tossing salad for a crowd you can toss your washed greens in a large plastic bag? Gently shake to mix and store in the refrigerator. It uses less space than a bowl and bagged salad is perfect for picnics and camping trips.

• For the crunch of cashews or peanuts and without their cost, shake on "nature's nuts," the seeds of papaya and fresh pomegranates. After you eat the fruit, dry-roast the seeds in a 300° oven until crunchy. You can toss them into tomorrow's cold salad.

• And to rid a garlic press of rancid garlic odors? Press through a wedge of lemon or lime, rind and all, and rinse.

• What tastes like pineapple, papaya, banana and strawberries all in one? The kiwi, a pale green high-C fruit with edible seeds. Let ripen until soft, peel, slice and toss in any salad.

• Putting figs in your chicken salad? Make them organic. Consumption of even small amounts of the sulfur dioxide used to treat dried fruit can destroy B complex vitamins and cause allergic reaction. Sulfur dioxide is also used to conceal defects in fruit. And although it's not as toxic, potassium sorbate, another common preservative used in processing dried fruits, may cause mild irritation to the skin. If you can't find organic, second best is sun-dried.

• Feed your salad with a fruit that's a vegetable—rhubarb. It has more potassium and fewer calories (20 per cup) than a navel orange. And rhubarb juice in your salad dressing provides triple your required daily allowance for B complex, the vitamin group that promotes healthy nerve tissues.

• Make a banana split salad for the kids. Bananas provide twice as many energizing carbohydrates as grapefruit, apricots or watermelon, and are a non-acid source of vitamin C (20 mg. per fruit).

• Try a fruit salad instead of fruit pie for dessert. A bowl of blueberries and mixed greens has 60 percent fewer calories than a fast-food fruit pie and 252 fewer milligrams of sodium. Or combine blueberries, blackberries or raspberries with beets or carrots.

MAIL ORDER SOURCES

Balducci's
424 Avenue of the
    Americas
New York, NY 10011
(212) 673-2600

• Gourmet salad ingredients

Walnut Acres
Penns Creek, PA 17862
(717) 837-0601

• Natural foods from herbs to nuts

Heller Enterprises
East Rockaway, NY
(516) 593-3557

• Whipped creams, sour creams, milk substitutes

Now Foods
721 N. Yale
Villa Park, IL 60181
(312) 833-4460

• Unusual seeds, nuts, herbs, fruits, vegetables for eating

Nichols Nursery
1190 N. Pacific Highway
Albany, OR 97321
(503) 928-9280

• Common and uncommon lettuce, herb seeds

Epicure Seeds
P.O. Box 450
Brewster, NY 10509
(unlisted phone)

• Common and uncommon lettuce, herb seeds

Frieda's Finest, Inc.
P.O. Box 58488
Los Angeles, CA 90058
(213) 627-2981

• Unusual seeds, nuts, herbs, fruits, vegetables for eating

Franjoh Cellars
Box 7462
Stockton, CA 95207
(800) 344-3221

• Vinegar-making kits

American Orsa, Inc.
75 N. State
Redmont, UT 84652
(801) 529-3526

• Natural Trade Mineral, a rock salt chemical and additive-free

Williams-Sonoma
P.O. Box 7456
San Francisco, CA 94120-
    7456
(415) 652-9007

• The works for cooks—from salad dryers to food items, like balsamic vinegar

INDEX